Love in the marketplace—who would have thought it possible? When Kevin Roberts' groundbreaking book *Lovemarks: the future beyond brands* was launched, brands were being smothered by over-management, blinding competition, and an explosion of choice. A powershift was occurring between producers, retailers, and consumers, resulting in the emergence of what Roberts has identified as the Attraction Economy. The effect of dropping the L-word into the world of business was electric. Reactions ranged from emotionally inspired to intellectually inflamed. From consumers, the response has been an outpouring of energy and enthusiasm for the products, places, and people they love. *The Lovemarks Effect*, the latest offering by Roberts, explores the fresh and exhilarating terrain created by Lovemarks. *The Lovemarks Effect* brings together the most engaging and insightful ideas and stories. It offers in-depth commentary from business, science, and creative luminaries who have been engaged in, and affected by, Lovemarks' power to make a difference in the world. Collectively, their voices emphatically support Roberts' central premise: the consumer owns the brand. Once consumers have tasted the freedom of Lovemarks they will become more creative, more engaged, and more involved. The next five years will change the face of business as we know it. The Lovemarks revolution is underway.

the lovemarks effect

WINNING IN THE CONSUMER REVOLUTION

KEVIN ROBERTS CEO WORLDWIDE, SAATCHI & SAATCHI, IDEAS COMPANY

 powerHouse Books Brooklyn, NY

love for Lovemarks

"In *Lovemarks: the future beyond brands*, Kevin Roberts, CEO Worldwide of Saatchi & Saatchi, aims to answer his own self-set question: what comes after brands? Through his work at companies including Mary Quant, Procter & Gamble, Pepsi-Cola, and Saatchi & Saatchi, he has perfected a marketing ideology that will solve this consumer conundrum. Basically customers must fall in love with a brand in order to stay loyal to it." *The Daily Telegraph*

"Ideas move mountains, especially in turbulent times. Lovemarks is the product of the fertile-iconoclast mind of Kevin Roberts, CEO of Saatchi & Saatchi Worldwide.

Roberts argues vociferously, and with a ton of data to support him, that traditional branding practices have become stultified. What's needed are customer love affairs. Roberts lays out his grand scheme for Mystery, Magic, Sensuality, and the like in his gloriously designed book Lovemarks." Tom Peters

"Roberts has managed to focus on that special something that everybody secretly wants, but over the years has given up on—to feel special, unique, loved, respected. He's not only determined it, he lives it. Roberts hands us on a silver platter the only tangible solution today to handle globalization, and that is to give each brand a Lovemark,

and each consumer the feeling that they can relate to a special something in a brand that describes the most important thing to them, themselves." *Arab-Ad*

"Finally, a new book from a respected ad man that captures the essence of brands and where they intersect with great advertising. Lovemarks is an exquisitely designed book whose layout is as engaging as the overarching themes Roberts has woven through the text." *Chicago Sun-Times*

"Lovemarks sounds simple, it looks simple, it is simple. Perhaps, but no one has ever laid it out so well and so plausibly as Kevin Roberts. A Lovemark doesn't have

to be a brand. It can be anything, as long as it stirs the emotions. Brands don't have any choice, according to Roberts: they must stir emotions or lose out. In no time at all Roberts has become a phenomenon." *De Standard*

"An entertaining, elucidating, and ultimately inspiring vision of the rejuvenation of brands through the power of love and the responsibility of business to fulfill one of its key functions—to make the world a better place." Editors' Selection for Best Business Books of 2004, Amazon.com

"Kevin Roberts doesn't dress like an ordinary CEO. Most important, he doesn't think like an ordinary ad

man. The transformation (beyond brands), Roberts says, requires a new set of ideas not only about brands, advertising, and marketing, but also about leadership, authenticity, and the human spirit." *Fast Company*

"Many people in the advertising industry, and many of their clients, do worry that brands—from packaged foods to luxury goods, from cosmetics to cars—have lost their hold on consumers, who are exposed to several thousand commercial images or messages every day. There is some hard-edged business reasoning behind Roberts' message. He is a persuasive spokesman for change." *International Herald Tribune*

For Ro—From Tolworth Broadway to St. Tropez.
Kids like us...baby we were born to run.

Contents

The new consumer

LOVEMARKS AND THE CONSUMER REVOLUTION

Everyone in business is experiencing the impact of the consumer revolution. The idea of Lovemarks was inspired by the desire to respond to this radical shift in what consumers need and desire. The new consumer is no longer willing to passively accept whatever comes their way from producers. Welcome to the challenge of the Attraction Economy—the ability to entertain, satisfy, and surprise consumers across the wide range of their tastes and passions.

It turns out that Lovemarks and the Attraction Economy were made for one another. This book is a record of how Lovemarks have been taken to heart by business and consumers.

MYSTERY SENSUALITY INTIMACY

We first presented Lovemarks in the September 2000 issue of *Fast Company*. Back then I was talking Trustmarks, but a bottle of great Bordeaux turned Trust into Love. We've never looked back.

Taking the first Lovemarks book to the world has been a fantastic ride—the response has been unbelievable. In China I talked with students who grabbed at Lovemarks like a life jacket. China is changing and these kids got it right away. Any real change will come from new ideas like Lovemarks, not rehashed versions of old ones. They saw that Lovemarks means transformation, not incremental improvement.

Their response was echoed everywhere. We'll have editions of *Lovemarks: the future beyond brands* (powerHouse Books, 2004) in 16 languages by the time you read this, and we have people from 149 countries registered at lovemarks.com. I was so energized by the whole experience, and the response was building so swiftly, that I knew we had to publish a new book fast, one that showcased what had been happening since we published *Lovemarks*.

The big news is that Lovemarks works in the marketplace. You can see it in the growing community on lovemarks.com, you can feel it in the responses we get from clients, and you can taste it in the numbers crunched in Lovemarks research. We have proven, once and for all, that Lovemarks are guaranteed profit generators and unbeatable consumer attractors. Tools like the Love/Respect Axis enable Inspirational Owners to examine their businesses and develop transformational ideas. Insights developed from the Love/Respect Axis allow leaps of the imagination that can result in new and powerful combinations. To find out how Lovemarks can transform real businesses we talked with a wide range of Inspirational Owners. The stories of these CEOs and senior marketers show a deep understanding of their consumers and an unwavering belief in the power of emotional connections.

Make way for

Lovemarks thinking has transformed Saatchi & Saatchi from an advertising agency into an Ideas Company. It inspires us to take our talents and passions in new directions. That's why you find us creating and managing a live band in the UK and working with many creative partners to create astonishing experiences like the Lexus interactive billboard in Times Square.

Lovemarks in business

It's not only Saatchi & Saatchi who have been putting the Lovemarks philosophy to work. I have been delighted to see Love become a welcome guest in the world of marketing. This is a big step up from when I used to mention the "L-word" and CEOs slid under their boardroom tables. Love is here to stay. Emotional connections with consumers are an irrefutable differentiator in the market.

Early on in the story I took the three vital Lovemarks elements—Mystery, Sensuality, and Intimacy—to the auto industry. For Lovemarks to work it had to be able to survive in one of the toughest, most macho businesses in the world. I looked out at a sea of guys at the J.D. Power 12th Annual Automotive Advertising Strategy Conference in California and told them that "moving metal" was an abysmal description of selling cars. "Don't tell your customers how much metal you move," I said. "Tell them how much the metal moves *you*." Suddenly these tough car guys realized that what they felt for the beautiful creatures they sold was Love.

I've seen the auto industry, more than any other, take up the powerful imagery and messages of Love and Lovemarks. Take a look at their most recent car advertisements—the emotions of ownership have replaced the conventional listing of benefits. Everywhere I see the word love—on billboards, in television commercials, and in print. At one stage there were so many hearts in newspapers and magazines it was like a Valentine's Day rash. Thank goodness people are now digging deeper and seeing that the heart is just one symbol of the Lovemarks connection.

Why would we discard emotions in business when they play such a central role in our daily lives? The same human impulses that create passionate connections in families and friends are the very ones we also need at work.

consumers!

The consumer and me

Nothing tests your commitment to Lovemarks more than whether you can accept that your brand belongs to the consumer. It isn't easy, but when a business takes this simple idea to heart, the results are startling. If you dispute the shift in power to consumers, think about this: since the first Lovemarks book was published in 2004, media that is supported, purchased, and controlled by consumers—like DVDs, computer games, and the Internet—has greater market share than traditional media supported by advertising. The move to consumer control is a thrilling challenge for business this century, and the winners will create new and exciting Lovemarks that can both turn the heads of consumers and warm their hearts.

Wherever consumers gather, Lovemarks live a charmed life. The consumer-Lovemarks combination is making the in-store shopping experience the great new frontier of Lovemarks. The new breed of stores will create a Theater of Dreams, and I'm not just talking about small-scale, high-end boutiques. The Theater of Dreams will be created wherever and whenever shoppers are in action. This is what will transform shoppers into buyers.

Screens playing heroic moments from great sports events, shoes displayed like works of art, and assistants who totally understand about putting the consumer in charge. This magic will be the foundation of a true Lovemarks shopping experience.

From irreplaceable to irresistible

To create a Lovemark is to make the transformation from being irreplaceable to irresistible. This is the only way we can succeed in what I call the Attraction Economy, a place where all companies must create powerful emotional experiences that turn the dreams of consumers into reality. From designing products to serving behind a counter to displaying goods in-store to telling stories for television. It is a challenge and an inspiration.

Commitment to Lovemarks is just a beginning. As consumers have become more confident that they own Lovemarks, they have demanded that the conversation with them becomes two-way. Only with Mystery, Sensuality, and Intimacy will businesses be able to create the compelling emotional experiences that will differentiate them in the marketplace and attract the Love of consumers. Forever. KR

CHAPTER ONE

L is for Lovemarks

BEGINNINGS

An introduction to the transforming potential of Lovemarks—how they have been taken up, their emotional impact, and how consumers have responded.

Insight interviews
Alan Webber, Co-founder,
Fast Company

Maurice Lévy, Chairman and CEO,
Publicis Groupe

Love bites
Backchat
Five things to do tomorrow

NUTELLA
My favorite uncle—
the impossibly handsome,
intelligent, cosmopolitan, and multi-
lingual Jimmy—used to bring me a jar
of Nutella from France each time he
visited home. Not only do I adore its
glorious chocolatey goodness, silk-velvet
texture, and that accessible-as-peanut-
butter-but-way cooler image, but it's like
having my favorite uncle with me again, hearing
him call me Megoo and admonish me to study
French. Nutella was his way of making sure I
stayed curious about the world beyond my
small Ohio town. It worked.
Megan, United States

Lovemarks in a nutshell

When I joined the advertising business in 1997 I arrived as an ex-client. I knew the problems facing brands throughout the world. Eventually the differences in price, packaging, and performance become so slight that these days only brand managers can tell the difference.

Back then I could see that even great brands were in danger of becoming commodities lacking differentiation. I looked at brands that escaped the commodity trap. Sure, some were small companies, but they had all tapped into something unique. In the end the answer, like most good ideas, was simple: people loved them for the long term. The consumers of these brands were Loyal Beyond Reason.

It was a matter of unearthing the roots of this tight bond. We soon discovered three key ingredients—Mystery, Sensuality, and Intimacy—and evolved the tools and processes you will find at work in the following pages. In this chapter Lovemarks is distilled to its essence. For the extended version check out *Lovemarks: the future beyond brands*.

Lovemarks revisited

Lovemarks are the brands, events, and experiences that people love. Not just like or admire, but love—passionately. Only Lovemarks explain why some brands enjoy enduring emotional connections. We're at the end of a journey that has taken us from products to trademarks, from trademarks to brands, and will now propel us from brands to Lovemarks.

Before any of this happens, however, a brand must build up huge reservoirs of Respect. Without Respect a brand too easily risks becoming a short-term fad or an unloved commodity. All great Lovemarks rest on a solid foundation of performance, innovation, reputation, and honesty. Without these values to center it, there can be no Lovemark.

The combination of three qualities separates Lovemarks from brands: **Mystery**, **Sensuality**, and **Intimacy**.

Mystery draws together stories, metaphors, dreams, and symbols, and is where past, present, and future become one. Mystery is also what keeps long-term relationships alive. The surprise party, the unexpected gift, the secret

Love Bridge

To launch Lovemarks *in Bulgaria Saatchi & Saatchi decked a pedestrian bridge in Sofia with hearts for five days in June 2004. Visit lovemarks.com/ launches/sofia for the full story.*

Launch of the Lovemarks *book at Club Love, Rio de Janeiro, Brazil.*

gesture. People love the spark of curiosity, the thrill of the unknown. After all, if we know everything, there is nothing left to catch us unawares and delight us.

Sensuality keeps the five senses on constant alert for new textures, intriguing scents and tastes, wonderful music, and spell-binding imagery. Our senses work together to alert us, lift us, transport us. When they are stimulated at the same time, the results are unforgettable. It is through the senses that we experience the world and create our memories.

Intimacy invokes empathy, commitment, and passion—the small, perfect gesture. These are the close connections that win intense loyalty and are remembered long after features and benefits have faded away. Without Intimacy people cannot feel they own a brand, and without that attachment a brand can never become a Lovemark.

Lovemarks and emotion

Lovemarks make it clear that when it comes to making decisions, people think with their hearts. People are about 80 percent emotional and 20 percent rational. Neurologist Donald Calne sums it up: "The essential difference between emotion and reason is that emotion leads to action, while reason leads to conclusions." More emotion, more action!

Lovemarks are the charismatic brands that people get emotional about, and they can be anything—from motion pictures to motorbikes, soap to shoes, cereal to cities. Take away a brand and people find a replacement. Take away a Lovemark and people protest.

The powerful emotional attraction of Lovemarks is what produces Loyalty Beyond Reason. This is the Loyalty that binds long-term relationships. It is not rational—it's a feeling, an emotional response. It is the sort of Love that can forgive lapses and understand failures. As we know from our own lives, when there is little to keep us together, Love often stops us from drifting apart. In a world where the growth of consumer choices has been exponential, loyalty has immediate bottom-line value. Psychologist Dr. Aric Sigman tells us that "people now have to make more choices in a single day than a caveman did in a lifetime."

You can feel this choice mountain casting a growing shadow across the freedom of your daily life. Around 6,500 songs on the average iPod, up to 50,000 items in an average supermarket, about 100,000 books in a typical Barnes & Noble. Have we time to choose between the 83 shampoos, 68 shower gels, and 77 washing powders we find on our supermarket shelves? Not in this lifetime. The prize will go to the shampoo, shower gel, or washing powder that makes an emotional connection with its consumers. Once that's done the competition will fall away.

Love/Respect Axis

The Love/Respect Axis is a fast way to separate Lovemarks from brands, fads, and commodities. Remember—to be a Lovemark you must start with high Respect. No Respect, no Lovemark.

Low Respect, Low Love

This is where consumers place the products they're not attracted to. They are tough critics who act on both emotion and reason. They sense there are major differences between their Lovemark and its competitors, although they often find it hard to explain exactly what they are. For a brand to escape this quadrant means getting emotional as well as addressing performance problems.

Low Respect, High Love

The fad zone is where you are a hero today and zero tomorrow. You know what I'm talking about—shaved heads, holidays in Libya, mobile phone ear pieces. But don't forget that what starts as a fad can sometimes win Respect and take its place as a Lovemark. Some parts of the games industry are making that journey right now.

High Respect, Low Love

This is where most major brands are stuck. Solid products and service but fixed on the "-er" words—brighter, stronger, faster, cheaper. In today's competitive world functional benefits have become table stakes. Consumers expect nothing less, and they want more.

High Respect, High Love

Lovemarks. This is the goal for all brands—to add Love and emotion to solid Respect for performance. High Respect may give you loyalty, but for the long term you need to go beyond reason, to Love. This is where everyone wants to be and stay. Fantastic quality, seductive attitude, irresistible appeal.

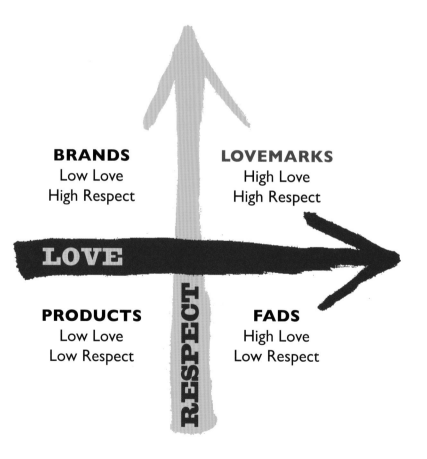

BRANDS
Low Love
High Respect

LOVEMARKS
High Love
High Respect

PRODUCTS
Low Love
Low Respect

FADS
High Love
Low Respect

LOVE

RESPECT

The future of Lovemarks

Lovemarks can be found everywhere, but in the Attraction Economy two places matter most: on-screen and in-store.

LOVEMARKS ON-SCREEN

In the 21st century the number of screens in our lives keeps growing—mobile phones, computers, PDAs, digital billboards, and television everywhere. In this world of screens consumers can instantly connect and interact with the products they care about online or on mobile phones. They have new ways to prove that they own brands as they make their own images and stories, create their own commentaries, and share experiences. Consumers have unprecedented opportunities to show Loyalty Beyond Reason and they are making the most of them.

As screens multiply and connect, we need a new word to describe this new world. For me, that word is sisomo. sisomo is the new power of Sight, Sound, and Motion on-screen. sisomo has the power to attract and engage. sisomo opens a new playground of opportunities. sisomo has fantastic potential to create emotional connections and Lovemarks.

LOVEMARKS IN-STORE

Mystery, Sensuality, and Intimacy are transforming the in-store experience. As they become Theaters of Dreams, stores will host the next creative revolution. Lovemarks in-store activate the drama of the brand where it matters by looking through the eyes of shoppers. It is in the store that over 80 percent of shopper decisions are made and 50 percent of switching between brands happens. The reality is that most people don't head to the store with a list they stick to. Decisions on what to purchase are very emotional. They're shaped far more than we realize by sensual displays and packaging, events and experiences, and imaginative groupings on the shelf. If you don't win the shopper's heart in-store, you will struggle to win it anywhere. KR

Sweet spot...

Alan Webber holds a special place in the history of Lovemarks. It was after a great discussion with him that the concept came together. I remember phoning him at some terrible hour of the night to tell him I'd cracked the name, and it wasn't Trustmarks! Alan, to his credit, took my enthusiasm in his stride and has been a great Lovemarks supporter ever since. Here he speaks with characteristic enthusiasm. KR

Learning Lovemarks

One of my first jobs after I graduated from college had nothing to do with the world of business. It was in the world of politics. I fell in with a guy who was, at age 29, the youngest big-city mayor in the United States—he was mayor of Portland, Oregon. What I saw him do, I realize in retrospect, was run his political office exactly the way Kevin talks about Lovemarks. You really have to listen to your audience, your consumers, and have a dialogue with them—and you've got to be incredibly mindful of their interests, you've got to be authentic with them at all times. Running for office was essentially about going beyond mere trust.

So when Kevin started talking about Trustmarks, and then enlarged that to Lovemarks, my reaction was—boy, that really creates a vocabulary for something that I experienced in my working life.

Lovemarks in action

The thing Lovemarks has going for it is a mindset that says, "Here's an emotional connection that changes the game." If you genuinely believe that your link to your audience—through the product, the communication, or the conversation—is from the heart, you have to behave differently. It's how you listen, how you respond and relate, and what you feel toward the person on the other side of the conversation.

One of the things we've always believed at *Fast Company* is that there is a higher road for business to take—that when you combine the notion that work is personal with the idea that performance matters, and you hook those two values up to the same energy source, you get the best of all possible worlds. I believe there's a sweet spot that combines the passion of your heart with the arithmetic of your wallet, and if you can find that sweet spot, then you're going to do great work.

Starbucks does it well. They've done a huge number of things right in how they relate to their product, their employees, and their consumers. I have a lot of friends who complain that Starbucks is to the coffee industry what Microsoft is to the computer industry. They think it's ubiquitous and that it's ruined the little coffee shops. My take on it is the exact opposite. Starbucks shows how a big company can still make small and meaningful gestures to its consumers. The Starbucks experience has managed to create personal intimacy where so many other large companies can only deliver formula responses. They've created an experience that totally transcends the product—and they've done it all over the world.

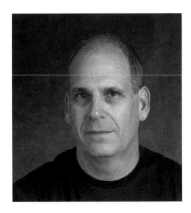

Alan Webber—who as co-founder of Fast Company, reinvented the way we think about business magazines.

I'm told that the highest volume Starbucks in the world is in Shibuya in Tokyo. This is partly a result of real estate, but it's a lot more than that. What they've done is create a haven. It's much more than just a cup of coffee. What they sell is an experience that they wrap around the coffee. It's such a powerful experience that it can make Americans feel more comfortable paying $3.50 for a cup of coffee than for a gallon of gasoline.

The economics of emotion

It's interesting that a Nobel Prize has been awarded to a couple of economists who demonstrated that emotion is a key element of economics. We all like to think that economics is cut and dried and that its laws are intractable, but we now have the Nobel Prize for Economics recognizing that, fundamentally, people live by their emotional reactions. It turns out that emotions are one of the key elements of their discipline. It's not about the cost per thousand, or the rate you are charging for the product. It's the way it feels and the way it represents itself.

The power of language

One thing that continues to interest me is how, in terms of *Fast Company* stories, the language we invented around 1995 to describe what we were then calling the new economy sounds so dated today. It's a sign that the game just keeps changing. There is no permanence in the sense that once you get it right you live with it forever. If you said to somebody today, "Our company is trying to create a new group of change agents," they'd look at you like you were stepping out of a time warp. It just doesn't sound right.

What that says to me is that one of the important things creative people have to do is listen. You'd think that what creative people do best is talk, and that's what you want to hire them for—to talk *to* you or talk *for* you. The truth is, the important step that precedes everything else is good listening.

If you're trying to track what's going on in the world of business, the economy, politics, or anything else, what you need to do to set yourself apart is to listen carefully to what we as human beings are sounding like. Then you need to tap into the kinds of words and expressions that are significant at any given moment.

Whoever controls the language controls the debate. If you get the language right, if you can change the way an issue is framed, you can begin to woo people into thinking about things your way because language is so powerful.

The consumer is in charge

The idea that the consumer is in charge has been around for a long time. Years ago when I was at the *Harvard Business Review*, the mantra was: our customers are our most important asset. Every company had that in its annual report. The problem was, no one actually behaved that way. It's too easy, if you're an incredibly well-paid business executive, to say, "Of course our customers are in charge. Now, how are we going to get 'em to do what we want?"

The younger generation of consumers, people in their twenties and under, find the whole thing so self-evident they don't even talk about it—they just behave it. The message to business is, "Look, if you really want to get my attention, you've got to change your behavior. Don't just express it in your briefs to your ad agencies. Adopt a different model in how you relate to the market, the customer, the technology that the web makes possible. *Show* us a different mindset, don't talk about it."

A look into the future

We'll continue to see a couple of things happening simultaneously. Don't forget that for every action there's an equal and opposite reaction. The main thrust that everybody will be tracking is the consolidation and implosion of almost every category you can think of. That might sound like a mundane observation, but if you look at the world today, we have an overabundance of many things.

There are too many cars made per year, too many airplane seats flying around the world empty, too much telephone capacity being produced, too many square feet of office space. We have global overcapacity in virtually every industry you can think of.

It's easy to imagine a world where for the next few years, even with the highest levels of corporate performance, we'll have more consolidation and a winnowing away of competitors in any given industry category. At the same time, the equal and opposite reaction will be the opportunity for your corner coffee store to proliferate like grass between the toes of the giant!

les suppléments

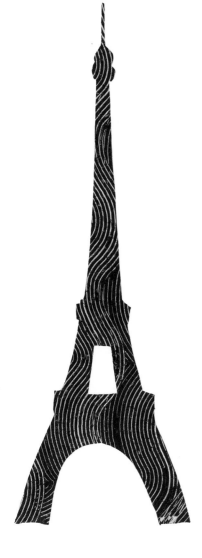

Saatchi & Saatchi is a member of Publicis Groupe, so I have a close partnership with Chairman and Chief Executive Maurice Lévy. One of Maurice's personal qualities is also one of his strongest professional ones: a respect for difference. He's tough-minded but, as his provocative ideas about communication and relationships show, his understanding of the value of emotional connections is profound. This is an extended version of the conversation with Maurice in Lovemarks: the future beyond brands. KR

On emotion

Consumers who make decisions based purely on facts are a tiny minority of the world's population. They are people without feelings, or perhaps people who put their heart and emotions in the fridge when they are leaving home in the morning, and only take them out again when they get home that night. But even these people buy some product or service based on impulse or emotion.

The majority of the population, however, consumes and shops with their mind and their heart, or if you prefer, their emotions. They look for a rational reason: what the product does and why it is a superior choice. They then make an emotional decision: I like it, I prefer it, I feel good about it.

The way this works is subtle. Most of the time, before seeing something in detail, you have a sense of what it is—before understanding, you feel. Making people feel good about a brand, getting a positive emotion, is key. This is what makes the difference.

It's very difficult to get emotion back into business in this period when cost-cutting is king. People making decisions are tense, under pressure, and rationality is reassuring. But emotions are more rewarding, both in the short and long term.

As I try to relate to all Publicis Groupe units and their positioning equitably, I do not personally use any of the methods developed by any single one of our agencies. But I can't help noticing that some brands are Lovemarks. Great brands that have become Lovemarks, even when they don't use the Saatchi & Saatchi methodology, all have a combination of Mystery, Sensuality, and Intimacy.

d'âme

Progression to Lovemarks

Moving from a brand to a Lovemark is, for me, changing the relationship between the consumer and the brand. This change is from a rational decision to buy a brand to an irrational, passionate decision to be loyal to that brand. You'll find that as the brand becomes a Lovemark, it will be forgiven for its mistakes—lack of innovation, perhaps not always the best timing or the best price.

In a Lovemark, the bond between the brand and the consumer is very strong. It has moved from a rational "I'm buying this because of this or that" to "I'm buying this because I really love it." It is adding to something that we call in France *les gratifications psychologiques*. It's giving you something that we call *les suppléments d'âme*—supplementing the soul. Now you can build loyalty with the consumer, which goes far beyond what you can get by being a brand, or even a mega-brand. It's a fantastic step to take.

Maurice Lévy—Chairman and CEO of Publicis Groupe, the fourth-largest communications group in the world.

Holistic communication

Better than any other brand, a Lovemark can use holistic communication and transmit messages through environments which are different. Lovemarks can permeate people's lives in various ways without being intrusive, and most of the time they are welcomed. The holistic approach is definitely a Lovemark approach.

As a corporation your brand is your most important asset. The value of the brand is much bigger than the value of the factories, the formulas, or the technology. Now corporations recognize the value of the brand, and on many balance sheets it is valued in billions.

Satisfying consumers

The world is becoming complex, so it is difficult today to optimize marketing communication and distribution. There are so many channels, so many mediums, so many ways of communication. This evolution has made marketing much more complex.

> ## When you're connecting you can bond, and you can move to the ultimate stage, which is the Lovemark.
>
> MAURICE LÉVY

Look at the evolution of how people think about consumption. After World War II if you satisfied consumers' needs they were happy. Marketing was relatively easy. But now they want something more sophisticated. Today consumers already have TV, they have two cars in the family, if not three. What we need to do is to bring something which is more about their psychological state of satisfaction—something that not only fills their needs but goes beyond them.

Service has nothing to do with price range. On the contrary, you might expect a cold approach from a high-class shop where you spend a great deal of money, but expect a warm approach from the bar or the grocery shop you go to on a weekly basis.

The power of the local

Because I am European, the idea of building Europe is very important. It is a dream. But the more we move towards something which is supranational, the more we'll go back to our roots. This is not only a European phenomenon, you see it everywhere in the world. What is this telling us? That deep down, in their minds, hearts, and souls, people want to go back to their cultures. They want to protect their roots. Not in the soil, because this concept is probably outdated, but in traditions and in culture.

There are no global consumers

At the head office–level you can control the definition of the brand, the positioning of the brand, and the communication model of the brand. Then you have to adapt how you will communicate to make the brand relevant to the local consumers. Why? First, because there is no such thing as a global consumer. There's only the consumer in their village, in their home, in their office, in their city.

Second, you have to make the brand mean something to them because they are different. They have their own specifics, they look at life differently, they have different incomes, different kinds of lives. If you want to penetrate the market deeply, you have to be in tune with these consumers. You need to communicate in a way that means you are connecting. When you're connecting you can bond, and you can move to the ultimate stage, which is the Lovemark. If you want to do that, you have to do it respectfully, by getting into the culture of each country.

The song of my mother

If I sing you the song my mother sang to me when I was a baby, it won't tell you anything. But it will bring tears to a lot of people in my region. If you cry too, it's nice, but not the same. It won't create the same vibrations in your heart, in your feelings, in your senses.

A final word on Lovemarks

Lovemarks has clearly caught the attention of the advertisers. They are interested in it. They want to understand how it works. They have clearly understood that being a Lovemark is the ultimate position from which to gain consumer loyalty.

BACK

The concept of Lovemarks has produced a wide range of responses from consumers. Perhaps it tapped into something that they knew all along and were waiting for marketers to discover. Whatever the reason, lovemarks.com has received a steady stream of comments from people who have something to say about the power of Love in the marketplace and in their lives. Their comments on how Lovemarks can be shaped, why some stories have more resonance than others, and how we could make the site more effective for them, are proof to us that consumers are one of the great untapped resources of modern business. Here is a sample of their insights, ideas, and observations. KR

Intuitively Lovemarks cuts to the core of business transactions: people do business with people. Therefore human emotions and drivers are touched and impacted. The human element of doing business is the hardest thing for a growing corporation to maintain.
Dave, NEW ZEALAND

The ability of a Lovemark to be successfully implemented is directly related to the activities of the organization providing the product or service. Marketing professionals should look into corporate reputation to gather a greater understanding of the non-marketing factors that will affect your ability to successfully implement a Lovemark.
Kim, AUSTRALIA

I really like the idea, it works logically, and I can see how Lovemarks supercede brands. But unfortunately it won't catch on—it is the wrong name. Change that and you have a winning concept!
Steven, UNITED KINGDOM

I don't think brands have lost their juice, but the juice is now expected to come out of different fruit. Some argue that customers surround themselves with brands and intangible attributes for social perception and self-recognition. I am sure of the contrary: people will more and more claim existence through social and ethical values and behaviors, and trust brands that are not only positioned as such, but that really act this way.
Manelik, SWITZERLAND

One thing I don't understand: Love works best when it goes two ways, is reciprocated. I can't see, therefore, that Love can ever describe what happens between me doing the buying and an organization doing the selling. Maybe I can love it, but they don't love me. They're just pretending, so they can make more profit from me.
JK, AUSTRALIA

CHAT

Consumers talk back about the idea of Lovemarks

Brand, Lovemark, whatever. Organizations that create great experiences and impeccable customer service will always surface with the trendiest nickname. Harley-Davidson doesn't care what the marketing world is calling them, they're too busy creating great experiences for Hog owners everywhere. Place hard-working, ambitious, creative individuals in front of the customer as often as possible and you will assuredly be crowned with the next-generation nickname as soon as it is released.
Derek, UNITED STATES

Lovemarks provides a new and interesting spin on consumerism. Lovemarks.com has given me a chance to evaluate and express my relationship to the products and services which define my life and relationship to the world. Consumerism is inescapable. Congratulations for giving it a positive perspective and direction.
Marina, AUSTRALIA

Surely "ownership" is a contradiction to Lovemarks. To me, a Lovemark infiltrates society to its core; it is at one with the audience it serves, occupying a paradoxical—and therefore unique—position between externality and internality, making the implications of "ownership" redundant as a solely external force.
Chloe, UNITED KINGDOM

Lovemarks reach a new level of leading, influencing, and inspiring people. Very few people look at what they see and read with a critical or questioning eye. Most are vulnerable to the messages they are constantly exposed to. Consumers are only empowered and in control at a superficial level. At a societal level they are controlled by our culture of eternally striving for more.
Maria, NEW ZEALAND

I think what turns a brand into a Lovemark is reality. Brands must connect more effectively with real people. Customers are deserting brands that seem unrealistic or phoney, so brands that portray unrealistic or phoney lifestyles need to smarten up and become more real in order to become a Lovemark.
Hesham, EGYPT

We need to think about the regional perceptions of material ownership and its correlation with actual emotional benefits. The concept you're probably looking for is loyalty, and the fact that it has become an overused and redefined term makes it no less relevant.
Jacob, AUSTRALIA

Gather stories about your brand in which you can trace an emotional dynamic. What do these stories tell you about the heart of your brand?

Commission a designer to create an icon that will be the inspirational beacon for your product or brand.

Choose a brand you love. Decide on its smell, its taste, the song it would sing in the shower.

Select a commodity, and using Mystery, Sensuality, and Intimacy, create a plan to make it a Lovemark.

Test your favorite brand on the Love/Respect Axis. Brainstorm ideas on how you could move towards the top right-hand quadrant.

CHAPTER TWO

Living the dream

THE ATTRACTION ECONOMY

To attract the new consumer we need new ways of thinking and acting. A guide to how to win consumer hearts by attraction.

Insight interview
Jim Stengel, Global Marketing Officer, Procter & Gamble

Love bites
Lexus IS launch
Five things to do tomorrow

Bright ideas

PIXAR Okay, those fish in *Finding Nemo* are the coolest characters ever created. I am a fish fanatic who spends her days sculpting and painting my own homage to everything that swims. I love Pixar for the genius that goes into everything they do! *Edith, United States* • **BANG & OLUFSEN** Truly an illustration of the beauty that can unite art and technology. Take the earphones: a simple object that's both functional and aesthetically pleasing. Great design and use of materials make these earphones a unique investment. If only all the objects in the world could be both innovative and inspirational. *Liming, Canada* **CANON** Canon is the clear leader in this race for digital imaging. I've tried Sony and Nikon cameras, but when I look at the rich colors emanating from my Canon images, I go into sensory overload! They make memories technicolor. *Chen Yen, New Zealand* • **SONAR** When I was younger, I never dreamed I could do the things that I'm doing now with this software. Ten to 15 years ago I would have needed tens of thousands of dollars to do the same things in a studio, and some things that SONAR enables were not even possible back then. The tools used by professionals are all available to me in my home studio. SONAR is like an extension of my creativity. I am realizing my dreams of creating professionally-recorded music, and I have just had my first success with music placement in a recent Hollywood movie. *Mao, United States* • **KODAK** How incredible is it to look at a picture of my child at one minute old, and compare it to a picture of myself at one minute old? How incredible is it to look at the date on the back and notice the Kodak logo on both? George Eastman really knew what he was doing when he founded Kodak. It's the only Lovemark I look for when I want to preserve the best moments of my life. *Adrian, United States*

LOVEMARKS **NOMINATIONS**

Consumers— the main attraction

Dylan got it right, the times they are a-changin'. The challenge is to understand what these changes mean and respond to them as opportunities. The world of consumers has been transformed over the past 25 years and businesses have struggled to find what really makes a difference.

The Information Economy, the Attention Economy, the Knowledge Economy, the Experience Economy, and more. Each has tried to crystallize what matters in the market. Each has given us useful insights and ideas but they have not delivered long-term differentiation and sustainable value. The reason is simple. They are all creatures of mass production and mass marketing. They're all united by the way they relate to consumers. It is strictly us-to-them.

Manufacturers told consumers to sit up and pay attention. Then retailers used the same currency of attention. Promotional offers, danglers on shelves, anything to catch the eye and close a sale.

We have entered a new world that no longer belongs to business. Companies don't set the terms and conditions, consumers do. No one knows this better than Procter & Gamble's Global Marketing Officer, Jim Stengel. In this chapter he offers deep insights into the changing relationship between consumers and today's marketers.

As consumers sense their power in the interactive world of digital media, a new context for business is being created. The old mass market model is collapsing. The only currency now of any sustainable value is ideas that attract consumers—an Attraction Economy. It was the emerging shape of the Attraction Economy that was the reason we needed Lovemarks in the first place.

I believe the Attraction Economy is the natural habitat of Lovemarks. KR

Lovemarks in lights

Launch of the Lovemarks *book, Geneva.*

THE NEW WORLD OF CONSUMERS

ATTENTION ECONOMY

ATTRACTION ECONOMY

ATTENTION ECONOMY	ATTRACTION ECONOMY
Interruption	Engagement
Directors	Connectors
Shout	Entice
One-to-many	Many-to-one
High-powered messages	Engaging content
Reactive	Interactive
Larger than life	My life
Return on investment	Return on involvement
Big promise	Intimate gesture
What you need	What I want
Explanation	Revelation

The action in attraction

Attraction is emotion with purpose. It charms and fascinates. Attraction never pressures. No wonder the Attraction Economy inspires creative action in the consumer-led world we are now part of. In the Attraction Economy the consumer must be at the center, and creating Lovemarks must be the goal.

The idea of attraction was abandoned to tourism and theme parks as mainstream marketing headed in the other direction to targeting and tight controls. For some companies like Starbucks, Virgin, and eBay, attracting consumers rather than demanding their attention was second nature. Their amazing success has meant there are now signs that attraction is starting to be taken seriously everywhere. The traditional industries of media and marketing, retail, and advertising are struggling to reinvent themselves—and how they connect with consumers is at the heart of the struggle. Viral marketing, consumers making their own media, and the transformed store experience are just the beginning.

People will only respond when you touch their own personalities, dreams, and desires—when you understand what attracts them. Never has being in tune with consumers been so important. The ear is one of the key marketing tools of this new century. That, and the understanding that people are attracted not by what they want, so much as by who they are.

In the Attraction Economy, job number one is generating ideas and insights to draw consumers closer.

SEVEN IDEAS FOR THE
Attraction Economy

1 SURPRISE ATTRACTS DELIGHT

People love what is new and different, exciting and stimulating. Continual innovation keeps attraction alive. It can be as simple as a new flavored cheese at an in-store sampling, or on the scale of the global roll-out of a new mobile phone. To be successful both need to share an intimate understanding of their consumers, to go beyond simply meeting their needs to surprise and delight.

2 LIKE ATTRACTS LIKE

People aren't magnets. We are attracted to the familiar. That's why empathy is the wellspring of the Attraction Economy. Everyone has their own distinctive mix of tastes and desires. Nothing attracts more than showing an intimate understanding of what they value most. The amazon.com recommendation system is a fantastic example of empathy in action. My local newsstand putting aside the latest issue of *Sports Illustrated* for me because it has a rugby story in it is another.

3 LEAD WITH THE SENSES

Think of the five senses as the five fingers on the right hand of attraction. Rich fragrances attract, and so too do satisfying tastes and stimulating tactile environments. The ability to make emotional connections through the senses is at the core of the Attraction Economy.

4 GREAT DESIGN IS IRRESISTIBLE

The skills of display are the front line of attraction. Not only can they win attention, they can inspire attraction. This is the challenge of the store, where the extraordinary creativity displayed by fashion and style brands from Gucci to Bathing Ape is working its way into supermarkets and convenience stores. As well as irresistible environments, design also has the constant challenge of making intensely desirable products out of the mundane. James Dyson did it and attracted thousands of people to display with pride one of the household's previously hidden drudges—the vacuum cleaner.

5 INTERACTIVITY LEADS TO COMMITMENT

Attraction is a two-way process. People now expect to be able to interact with brands. An 800 number in tiny print on the label doesn't do it anymore. Lexus has been leading the way online by encouraging chat groups and communities, offering mobile phone rings, creating podcasts and streaming broadcasts to draw potential customers closer to the cars.

6 ENTERTAINMENT ATTRACTS CONNECTION

We all like to have fun, to feel engaged, to swap stories. The skills of the storyteller and entertainer animate the Attraction Economy. Throw out your preconceptions. A greater proportion of Generation Xbox is made up of women over the age of 18 (28 percent) than boys aged from six to 17 (21 percent).

7 MUSIC IS THE HEAVY LIFTER OF EMOTION

Humans have been finding themselves in music for over 30,000 years. Imagine the primal delight consumers have with their choices now. Music used to come in songs on albums where the selection of songs and the order to play them was set by the record companies. Now it comes in songs *and* albums. And music lovers are making the most of their new freedom to mix and match. In February 2006, the billionth song was downloaded from itunes.com.

> ## "The world is moving from mass media to my media."
>
> DAN ROSENSWEIG

Screens in the Attraction Economy

The inspiration of Lovemarks has always been making emotional connections with consumers. Finally technology is catching up. The screen has leapt out of the living room and into our pockets, our hands, our offices, cars, stores, and our streets.

Screens are huge players in the Attraction Economy. And they are morphing to be more, do more, inspire more. Television is becoming more game-like, mobile phones more television-like, in-store screens more movie-like, and computer screens—they are finally becoming possible to like.

Dan Rosensweig, COO of Yahoo!, sums it up perfectly: "The world is moving from mass media to my media."

According to Ball State University, ordinary, everyday Americans spend more of their time (around nine hours per day) using media than doing anything else. And today of course that media is mostly on screens—television, mobile phones, computers, games machines, MP3 players.

In the past 10 years we have seen screens rapidly get smart, mobile, and more connected. Strategy Analytics predicts that mobile companies will have around 50 million users of mobile television by 2009.

TRANSFORMING SCREENS WITH SISOMO

sisomo is a new word for the world of the Attraction Economy. Sight, Sound, and Motion are to the screen what Mystery, Sensuality, and Intimacy are to Lovemarks. And the word sisomo can talk in any language. It's a noun. It's a verb. It's an adjective.

sisomo brings screens to life in the Attraction Economy. On-demand, on-the-go, emotionally compelling ideas on-screen. In sisomo art meets science, emotion meets technology.

Sight, Sound, and Motion are the most powerful ingredients for making compelling communications. Humans love excitement. They revel in shape and color. They are passionate about music and find movement on screen irresistible.

> ## Everything is held together with stories. That is all that is holding us together, stories, and compassion.

HOLSTUN LOPEZ

It's great to see consumers finally moving into territory that has traditionally been dominated by techies. Even people who used to shy away from technology can make their own high quality sisomo and, more importantly, they have the chance to attract the world as their audience. Now consumers are getting into the action. On their computers and increasingly their mobile phones, consumers have taken control. They can research any product, compare it with the competition, find the best price, keep up-to-date, tell their friends, ask questions, complete the transaction.

sisomo gives companies the opportunity to differentiate products with engaging and entertaining screen experiences. With sisomo they can develop new channels that engage with what consumers have to tell them, to show them, to inspire them.

The big opportunity for sisomo in the Attraction Economy is to create new screen formats, new stories, new characters, and new ways for consumers to participate and communicate.

THE THREE ATTRACTIONS OF SISOMO
sisomo is everywhere

We're never more than an arm's length away from a screen. Sixty percent of people leave their mobile phones on when they sleep. The key is using this access to consumers wisely. The time for interruption and insistence is long gone. Movies and television demonstrated the positive powers of sisomo with compelling stories, entertaining ads, and thrilling sports. Now watch sisomo reach out to ever more screens in ever more surprising places. Where will we find these screens? Anywhere and everywhere the consumers want to watch and interact with them.

sisomo is interactive

For decades screens told consumers, "sit back and let us entertain you." Television and movies ruled the planet. Then screens began to invite consumers to "lean forward and get involved." Games and mobile phones, video gadgets and computer screens—from relaxing on the couch with TV after a day's work to opening new worlds of games, shopping, communication, and information. The average American household now owns around 25 consumer electronics products. Interactivity has moved far beyond being a fun extra.

sisomo tells stories

In the twenty-first century the status of stories is being transformed. Their ability to inspire people and to connect with consumers puts them at the heart of business. As the writer Holstun Lopez so astutely noted, "Everything is held together with stories. That is all that is holding us together: stories, and compassion." The art of sisomo is story-telling. Technology has unleashed amazing new opportunities to tell stories, to communicate, and to inspire. The growth of online sisomo is happening faster than most of us dreamed possible. Where once downloading a short sisomo clip was a major challenge of coordination and software compatibility, it is now just a click away.

The huge success of websites like youtube.com and videobomb.com demonstrates the attractions of the online sisomo revolution. Both have become venues for consumer-created sisomo from all over the world. Make a smart sisomo story that engages and compels and you can start a viral whirlwind—as well as sit back and wait for the job offers. sisomo stories are reinventing the formats that were set by television in the 1950s. Stories have never been so popular or so easy to share.

Who will get ahead in the Attraction Economy?

The winners in the Attraction Economy will be the brands that understand sisomo and aspire to be Lovemarks. As Inspirational Consumers become more active as marketers and advocates, as well as critics and judges, expect to see the art of attraction become central to business. Those companies that already understand that their role is to entertain, persuade, respond, and illuminate are already players in the Attraction Economy.

Now that consumers are walking away from the mass market, they want to get closer and get more personal. They want to talk as well as listen, to create and to have fun. The new consumer wants you to be in their heart, not in their face. KR

Always Moving

Our client Procter & Gamble is a truly global company. Three billion times a day their iconic brands like Tide, Pampers and Olay touch consumers. When P&G talks, people listen. In 2004 Jim Stengel, Global Marketing Officer for P&G, declared that the traditional mass marketing model was broken. Consumers were becoming less responsive to traditional media and embracing technologies that gave them more involvement. Jim saw that the future of marketing lay in attracting consumers, not in targeting them. Here he discusses how P&G is shaping this new marketing environment. KR

The main attraction

The concept of the Attraction Economy absolutely describes what is happening. Every successful marketer or brand builder understands that we are only in the lives of consumers because they have invited us. We need to both respect and reward this invitation.

I recently visited our organization in South Africa and we have a program there that brings the principles of the Attraction Economy to life. Our feminine care brand, Always, did not have a very strong market share or the strongest equity with young women in South Africa. Then we made a genuine effort to understand the lives of teens better. What we learned is that there is a phrase they use: "Keep Movin'." In the new South Africa, post apartheid, this philosophy means that in order to realize your potential you need to Keep Movin'—continue with your education, grow with life, and do not be slowed down by drugs or early pregnancy. Be agile, dance—forward motion is what it's all about. We wanted to do something positive around this insight so we put this important message together with the activity of music and dance deeply engraved both in the African culture as well as in the teens' world. The result was the idea to sponsor the Always Keep Movin' Dance Contest. We had no idea of what we were uncorking! Thousands of girls entered. Local DJs, hip hop artists, and performers judged the competition by city, and then the best contestants competed on a network television show. As well, the Always Keep Movin' rap song became a national hit.

The program is in its infancy but we'll grow it and perhaps export it to other places with a strong dance culture. Why wouldn't it work in Brazil or in the United States? Now, this is really different marketing because we were doing something that was important and created attraction with teen girls. We were immediately relevant to them. And you know what happened? On Always our volumes went up, our equity scores went up, all our traditional measures went through the roof, and very fast. P&G is now making relationships with empathy and we are building our marketing understanding so we can connect on a different level. That's the Attraction Economy.

If you can create marketing that makes a difference in someone's life, then that's the gold standard. To reach that standard you have to be authentic. People really can see through you when you're not. Consumers care about who is behind brands and products. This is why your values matter. You can't do something just because you have to grow share by ten points or make your boss happy. You need a deeper sense of purpose and commitment. That is what has distinguished P&G over the decades. People join us because they believe in what the company stands for. We aim to touch lives and improve life, and that goes well beyond our products and services.

Opening up the conversation

All communication, all brand building, all relationships, all decisions, are emotional. If you're not in touch with that knowledge, if you're not dealing with that reality, then your brands will not connect with consumers.

One of the inspiring things about P&G over the last several years has been our focus on the "Consumer is Boss" model. We are changing the dialogue with the consumer and are more personally involved. Consumers appreciate the fact that we respect them and that we care about their opinions.

We've certainly opened up and gotten involved in many more conversations. Technology is now enabling us to connect with people one-on-one, and we are innovating with ways to do this. The trillion-dollar media question is, "when and where and in what forms will people be connected with one of their screens?" The connectivity of the world has exploded. The shift from attention to attraction, from proclaiming to involving, has occurred.

Jim Stengel—*as Global Marketing Officer for Procter & Gamble he has been described as "one of the marketing industry's key change agents."*

> ## "For someone who likes to think, and to collaborate, and to get personal with consumers, it's a great time to be a marketer. "
>
> JIM STENGEL

We're creating environments to attract people who are important to us. Tremor is our initiative in the United States for sharing new ideas and products with an online network of 250,000 American teens. We are upfront that this is a marketing service that develops teen word-of-mouth programs. In 2006 we launched Vocalpoint for Moms based on the same word-of-mouth principles. Mothers are very important to this company. We need to get into the right conversations with them. Already more than 500,000 Moms have signed up to be part of Vocalpoint.

We are finding that many of our products are in high-involvement categories where we can start new conversations. On a laundry brand like Tide one of the questions we ask Moms now is a big one: "What are your hopes for your children?" Whether you are in Beverly Hills or Bangalore, that question changes the conversation profoundly. Every mother shares the same desire for her children to live a better life, however differently they might express it. We don't go in and start with, "How's Tide doing on your stains!"

Mr Clean gives another example of the power of new questions. It was magic on floors but the brand didn't radiate this. We invited in world-class designers. They didn't ask how to make Mr Clean liquid work better or smell better. Instead they asked: "Can we find how to make cleaning more interesting?" That was a great question.

The future of marketing

As competition gets more intense, marketing becomes more creative, more interesting, and much more important. To do great marketing you have to create the right organizational culture, share good ideas, ask the right questions, and learn how to share inspiration.

I don't see any of our brands being defined today solely by functional value, but 10 years ago you could. Pampers was about dryness and Mr Clean was about clean floors. For us to get to Pampers being about a baby's development and Mr Clean being about astonishing consumers, whether it's with the Magic Eraser or the Magic Reach, has been a huge change.

I see my role as attracting the best agencies in the world to work with us – and then attracting the best talent to provide a very wide range of marketing expertise. We need diverse partners with diverse skills. Peter Sealey of the University of California at Berkeley uses a great analogy. It's no longer enough to be the "Masters of Marketing." We must become "Maestros of Marketing." That means being like the conductor of an orchestra guiding self-motivated specialists rather than following the command and control model.

Process will always be important. It's a core competency of P&G. We are very good at codifying what we know and then getting it around the world fast. And we will always value measurement. But we are learning and evolving. The companies who understand the consumer and their own business landscape, and who get the right people and unleash their creativity by bringing them together with one set of goals and one dream, they are the ones who get incredible results.

For someone who likes to follow a rulebook, it's a tough time. For someone who likes to think, and to collaborate, and to get personal with consumers, it's a great time to be a marketer.

The questions to ask are: What is your place in how consumers experience media? What is your place in-store? And, in some countries where sales are moving online, what's your place in that environment? It is a time of possibilities.

I don't think there is a marketing model any more. I think there is an approach and a discipline. To make emotional and relevant consumer connections you need great agility and you need to be experimental. You need an organization that has very creative approaches to marketing because there is not going to be a single way. There are going to be many different ways. If you have a superior organization with great consumer empathy, and you have the right kind of agencies to partner with you, then you'll figure it out. In the end it gets down to talent, culture, and values. If you know what you stand for and you are in touch with the consumer, the future is yours.

Always Keep Movin' Dance Contest, Durban, South Africa.

LEXUS IS: "WHY LIVE IN ONE DIMENSION?"

Here's sisomo at its best in a Times Square Lexus spectacular. An example of sisomo in action— consumer focused, entertaining and interactive. Team One's Brian Sheehan takes up the story. KR

To involve thousands of people with the launch the Lexus IS, Team One USA worked with the Venice Consulting Group and DHAP on a photo-mosaic website to produce an event that literally towered above Times Square in New York. People were asked to submit photographs online. With the help of VCG and DHAP around 80,000 images were used to construct a giant photo-mosaic of the new Lexus IS on the Reuters megascreen. People could also locate their own images in the Lexus IS mural using guidelines emailed to them. Using a random Flash technology zoom effect, individual images could be displayed over 32 feet tall. The Times Square mural certainly answered the Lexus campaign question, "Why live in one dimension?"

Find out from people under 20 what attracts them to video games. Apply their insights to your business.

If you can't send images and videos on your mobile phone, learn. Now.

Count the number of screens in your life. Now do you understand why this is the Screen Age?

Create a portrait of your brand in full sisomo. Does it resonate with people in the business? With consumers?

Learn to play at least one video game. Experience the attraction.

CHAPTER THREE

Planet Lovemarks

LOVEMARKS IN THE REAL WORLD

Lovemarks can play at many different levels, from the intensely personal to a leading role on the global stage. A look at Lovemarks through the eyes of Inspirational Consumers around the world.

Insight interviews

Richard Hytner, Deputy Chairman, Saatchi & Saatchi Worldwide

Malcolm Gladwell, author

Inspirational Consumers

Richard Vallens on Bike Friday

Philippe Lentschener, Vice President Europe, Saatchi & Saatchi, on FNAC

Love bites

Planet Lovemarks map
Lovemarks stories
Five things to do tomorrow

love in any language

AIR JAMAICA Air Jamaica is the airline of choice for my family. My sister first flew to America on The Lovebird in the Sixties and the rest of us have flown Air Jamaica ever since. It's a flying piece of Jamaican culture in its entirety—the music, food, service, and several Jamaican female pilots create a nostalgic ambience for ex-pats visiting home, and evoke the Caribbean courtesy and easy-going affability that tourists love. *Audrey, United States* • **LEGO** Lego never dies. Isn't it the simplest and yet the most complicated toy we've ever seen? Its limitless combination capacity inspired me then and its simplicity inspires me now. Thank you Lego, for being there for such a long time. *Gun, Turkey* • **PINK FLOYD** The ultimate Lovemark of my teenage years. For us kids behind the Iron Curtain, Pink Floyd's music and poetry was our secret way to remain sensitive and thinking people in times when being sensitive and thinking could mean persecution and repression. The refined magic worlds of Roger Waters, David Gilmour, and the other genius guys from Pink Floyd have helped me and many of my friends appreciate the beautiful and the sophisticated. *Plamen, Bulgaria*

PRORASO SHAVING SOAP No matter where I am or what bathroom I'm in, a tub of Proraso on the vanity makes it temporarily my own. The clunky green plastic container and the rich eucalyptus smell is familiar and reassuring. The morning shave ensures an enforced couple of minutes' quiet. The sound of the lid snapping back onto the tub ends the ritual and launches the day. *Mark, Australia* • **SCRABBLE** Love. Game. Interesting. Fun. Family. Playing. Enjoyment. Sunday. Afternoon. World. Words. Coffee. Fun. If I was in the middle of a game right now I'd be winning with this word: Lovemark. *Gustavo, Mexico* • **TINTIN** Hergé created Tintin with the fine attention to detail and craftsmanship that enables a new world of adventure to strike root and bloom in the imaginations of young children all over the world. The hours of wonder spent in the quests of Tintin and company have had a formative influence in shaping the quests of many a youth! *Avi, Israel*

Lovemarks, we think the world of you!

Like Lovemarks, this chapter belongs to the Inspirational Consumers of the world. The people who don't just understand that consumers are now in control, but do something about it. Inspirational Consumers react instinctively to Lovemarks, completely unprompted. It is their passion and enthusiasm that continually confirms my belief in the consumer revolution.

The world map according to lovemarks.com says it all—each pin on the map locates new points of view about the things people love. One of the fascinating aspects of the comments we receive is that people share a common voice. Whatever their first language, however large or small their homes, whichever currency they use to pay for their products, the language of Lovemarks is the shared language of human emotion. This is why we found that many of our Lovemarks stories, whether they be from Africa, Europe, or America, were grounded in common childhood experiences. This is completely in tune with the Lovemarks belief in Intimacy and the powerful combination of Mystery's past, present, and future.

The wonder of discovering a perfect tool, the joy of tasting a loved local delicacy, the pleasure of belonging are understood by human beings everywhere.

And what are some of the shared words that come to us from all parts of the globe? Timeless, magic, fun, passion, imagination, devoted, loyalty, memories, romance, friends, and of course love.

In this chapter Saatchi & Saatchi's Richard Hytner explains how, by gaining a deep understanding of these consumers, their passions can be introduced into the market place.

Of all the people who have participated on lovemarks.com, one of the most dedicated Inspirational Consumers is Richard Vallens. Richard won a Toyota Prius for his fantastic nomination of his Lovemark, Bike Friday, on lovemarks.com.

Malcolm Gladwell has a talent for capturing big and important ideas. He reminds us again that the heart rules the head and what this means for word-of-mouth and the tension between trust and expertise. KR

The Red Room

Launch of the Lovemarks *book, Sydney, Australia.*

RED PIN   PUSH PIN   HEART
1-100   101-500   501+

Planet Lovemarks

the lovemarks.com community

inspirational consumers

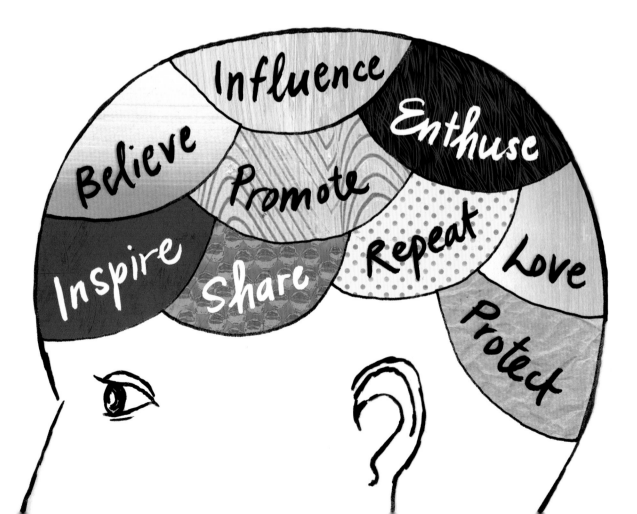

Lovemarks are based on the conviction that consumers are in control, which makes listening to them one of the great Lovemarks skills. They are no longer prepared to accept whatever is offered—and businesses are responding to these new, demanding consumers. Here's Richard Hytner, Deputy Chairman, Saatchi & Saatchi Worldwide, on the power of the Inspirational Consumer. KR

Proud to be passionate

Richard Hytner—*putting a face to Loyalty Beyond Reason.*

Time was when the only role of the consumer was to walk into a store, select her brand, and pay for it at the counter. Now consumers— informed and empowered by the Internet and liberated by their mobiles—are actively engaged in the way their favorite brands behave in the market place. This shift in attitude has been embraced by companies smart enough to treat their consumers as partners rather than end users.

Take Harley-Davidson. Its executives not only love riding their Harleys, they also love attending conventions and heading out on trail rides with other enthusiasts. Not surprisingly, this combination of empathy, curiosity, and partnership proves compelling to Harley lovers. Customer focus? More like consumer fellowship.

Global giants like our client Procter & Gamble also appreciate that the consumer is more than simply a funnel through which to pour their brands. P&G is creating intimate connections with consumers in the places where they work and live. P&G appreciates that what counts is how consumers interact with the brand. They take an anthropological approach to see first-hand how consumers use their products in the home, and apply these insights to make their products even more useful, respected, and loved.

Harley-Davidson and P&G understand that a new, energized consumer group has been born. Inspirational Consumers are the people who are ready and willing to intensify their interaction with companies. They are so passionate about the future of their Lovemarks that they don't hesitate to take action. They are determined not just to ensure that the brand stays true to its promises, but to effect change when it doesn't.

> **Inspirational Consumers love influencing other consumers as well as those who make the products they love.**
>
> RICHARD HYTNER

With the rapid increase and sophistication of digital communications, Inspirational Consumers are armed with ever-growing power to shape the market. What is the make-up of the Inspirational Consumer? And how would you know one if you saw one?

1. Inspirational Consumers are articulate

Inspirational Consumers fully understand the dynamic that moves brands to Lovemarks. They have no difficulty in adopting the language of Love and emotion; they have proved insightful at intimately connecting Lovemarks with their lives (just look at how users make pages at myspace.com their own). They are adept at describing their Lovemarks through compelling stories. They say what they feel rather than what they think. This is how they spread the word about their Lovemark.

Does this kind of informal communication actually work? The answer is yes. According to a study by researchers NOP World, 93 percent of those polled claimed they would take action if engaged by what NOP called a "specific word-of-mouth influencer." And to Inspirational Consumers, it's more than word-of-mouth. It's what they feel.

2. Inspirational Consumers are not content to keep Lovemarks all to themselves

Inspirational Consumers love influencing other consumers as well as those who make the products they love. What else explains the impetus behind the thousands of reviewers who promote or critique books on the pages of amazon.com? Some are so personally involved that they seal their reviews with their own photographs. What else would have energized George Masters to spend hours creating his very own Nike commercial celebrating golfing genius Tiger Woods, before sharing it on the web for everyone to see? It's this desire to share that has driven the development of open source software like Linux, now a global software force.

Inspirational Consumers have a halo effect. Their glow draws other people into the brand. Inspirational Consumers are the advocates, the shopping guides, and the unhidden persuaders.

3. Inspirational Consumers get deeply immersed

They cannot resist getting involved with the processes that help create their Lovemarks. Smart businesses have been quick to understand this passion. To expand their pool of expertise and ideas, Electronic Arts, makers of computer games, are delighted to draw on the creative energy of their Inspirational Consumers. The company sends them programming tools so they can participate in modifying and inventing games and putting them online. It is going to become increasingly critical for every R&D department to make more active connections with consumers and to tap into their creativity to make this happen.

4. Inspirational Consumers promote, rally around (and rage about) their brands

When Inspirational Consumers fall in love, the effect on brands is dynamic. But they are quick to remind "brand owners" of their responsibilities. You see this when local television channels try to change the time of a favorite television show. If the new time does not suit them, Inspirational Consumers will be quick to react. In fact, they'll just get the original schedule reinstated!

LOVEMARKS

A difficult game

Word-of-mouth becomes more and more important as the love of minor information grows in our society. It's a direct function of that.

MALCOLM GALDWELL

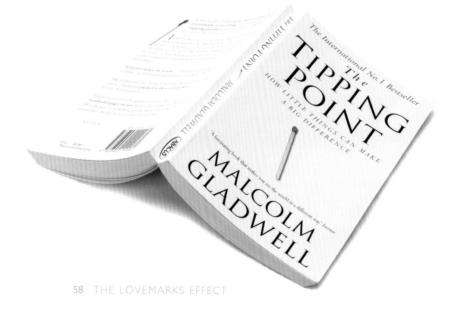

When he introduced the idea of the tipping point, Malcolm Gladwell not only produced an international best-seller, he also made a huge impact on business. KR

Malcolm Gladwell—TIME *magazine named him one of the 100 most influential people of 2005.* Fast Company *calls him "a rock star, a spiritual leader, a stud."*

Word-of-mouth

Word-of-mouth is a reflection of how we deal with information in our lives. It's a reflection of the type and volume of information. Word-of-mouth becomes more and more important as the love of minor information grows in our society. It's a direct function of that.

When you had only two toasters to choose from in 1955, you didn't need word-of-mouth to know which to buy—it was an obvious choice. It's a paradox of the information age that, as it grows more sophisticated and complex, the need for these basic points of communication grows.

In a weird way, the more books you have available to you, the fewer you read. The more choices that are available to you in the supermarket, the fewer choices you make. You react to being overwhelmed by narrowing your field of vision, not by embracing the increased number of choices. Whenever you narrow your field of vision, you're handing over responsibility for decision-making to trusted people in your life. That is the engine of word-of-mouth.

Word-of-mouth and advertising

Word-of-mouth is the submission of consumers. "Enough is enough," they say. It's them throwing up their hands and waving the white flag. Word-of-mouth is growing in importance to the point where a model of advertising for many brands in the future will be simply finding a way to reach people who are driven by word-of-mouth.

The mass element of advertising is going to diminish in importance. You can see it already in American television viewing patterns. People who watch *Sex in the City* aren't watching any advertising because it's on premium cable. I'm quite convinced that the same is true in the print media. The amount of advertising available is simply a blur, and the amount of recall of specific messages is minimal. When that happens information is communicated almost entirely informally and the rules change. Then word-of-mouth influencers become paramount.

Finding them is nowhere as easy as finding consumers we have traditionally considered influential. When we thought influentials were rich and well-educated it was dead easy to find them. When they have social skills that don't correlate with education and income, they become a lot harder to find. Now you're trying to find them through their patterns and it's a much trickier game to play—it differs from domain to domain. Some may be female and some may be male, and some may be old and some may be young. There's no question that it's a much more difficult game.

Trust versus expertise

There's a trade-off in word-of-mouth between trust and expertise. If I wanted to get the absolute best source on computers, I would find someone who worked in the industry. But if I don't know anyone who works in the industry who I also have a strong personal bond with, I've got a trade-off that affects every one of my consumer choices.

I tend to opt for trust over expertise, and I ask my brother. What I'm looking for is someone who is defined simply by knowing more than me and also by knowing me very well. This is as opposed to someone who knows me only moderately well, but knows an extraordinary amount about whatever I'm interested in.

A mistake businesses make is to assume that their consumers prefer their expertise to their trust. False! We are only looking for someone who has a marginal advantage over us in information. We make socially acceptable choices informed by someone we trust and knowing that they won't look down on us for making it.

Loyalty

I'm a loyalty skeptic. I don't think that it is as high on the list of consumer concerns as it is on the list of producer concerns. I also think that a lot of the time people see loyalty where loyalty does not exist. Often what looks like loyalty is simply habit or unthinking allegiance. The effect is the same but the condition is different. For instance I am happy with my Saab and I am loyal to the particular representation of Saab at this moment, but I would not have bought a Saab in 1987, because at that moment Saab was something that was very different. Similarly, I might have bought a BMW in 1975, but I would not buy a BMW today. BMW might think of itself as being a consistent entity over that period, but my social group's understanding of what the BMW means has changed.

Intuition

Blink is about what it means to take the unconscious seriously in marketing and decision-making. This is also a project which is consuming much of psychology at the moment. It is a kind of return to the unconscious after a gap of 50 years and in a much more sophisticated way. When you take the unconscious seriously you undermine virtually all quantitative market research and its focus.

This is great news for the creative part of the advertising world, and bad news for the number-crunchers and other unwelcome invaders into the world of marketing.

lovemarks stories

People everywhere have taken the opportunity to tell their stories on lovemarks.com. Over the years the site has grown into a fascinating resource of what matters to people. And they have shown themselves to be independent, passionate, well-informed, single-minded, and entertaining. Just like people in love.

The nominations cross all boundaries and come in all shapes and sizes. Everyday products, supermarkets, spiritual touchstones, luxury goods, tourism destinations, and popular culture—they're all there. I'm always astonished at the passion and commitment these consumers bring to the site.

Here are some of my favorites, pulled together from the ocean of love that is lovemarks.com. KR

Chanel No.5

This was my first perfume—my mum gave me one of those small sample bottles when I was eight. Every time I smell it, it reminds me of how naughty and grown-up I felt the first time I carefully took off the lid and dabbed on the scent, with my eyes closed, thinking that someone was going to fall in love with me the moment they smelled me. Romance, glamour, and hope in a bottle.

June, SINGAPORE

Diesel

I love Diesel because they've earned my respect. I'll never forget when I first saw their "Sailors" billboard—I was so proud that the brand I love was doing what no other brands dared. They aren't just another label saying you'll be transformed when you wear their clothes. They are genuinely irreverent, challenging the mass market, and that makes them cool. To top it off, their clothes are the perfect fit for my lifestyle. What more do you need? A true Lovemark.

Dieter, GERMANY

Coleman camping products

My family and I spent countless childhood weekends and holidays camping in Alberta. We were exposed to all forms of weather—usually on the same day. Sometimes the only ray of light on our trips was our boldly colored, highly reliable Coleman camping gear. From our coolers to our lantern to our two-burner portable stove, Coleman was there for us, never letting us down. My Coleman products have lasted as long as my uncompromising loyalty to them (I buy nothing else). How reliable is Coleman? Thirty years later I still have the cooler, the lantern, and the two-burner stove. They remind me of a special childhood full of memories and are still around to create new memories with each trip—now that's a Lovemark.

Craig, CANADA

Crayola crayons

Whether it's a simple, flat little box of eight colors, or a big box of 64 (with the sharpener in the back!), nothing smells more like childhood than the distinctive, warm, waxy scent of these crayons. Is there anyone who didn't create their first artistic masterpiece or learn how to spell their own name with a Crayola crayon clutched in their fist?

Eve, UNITED STATES

MAC

MAC evokes passion, fun, inspiration, drive, power, and the confidence to be different and express exactly who I am, when I want. I love MAC's enormous collection of colors and products to match every need, and cater to every culture and nationality—multiculturalism expressed through make-up. MAC matches my skin tone when no other brand can. I love MAC because MAC understands me.

Shobana, CANADA

LUXE city guides

Forget leafing through pages of outdated, uninspiring text, and arriving at your destination only to find it dreary, misrepresented, or shut. No longer will you have "tourist" slapped across your forehead as you dither around, confused, frustrated, and lost. The LUXE guides contain secrets that even the sassiest folks about town don't know. You will be cosseted, pampered, and revitalized, and you will laugh till your drawers drop. These guides condense each city into a glorious, golden nutshell. The LUXE guides are simply beyond the brand.

Grant, UNITED KINGDOM

Jo Malone

Despite her success Jo Malone's brand remains deeply intimate, true to its beginnings. From mixing unique face creams specifically for each of her clients in her flat 20 years ago to now, running an internationally successful business, Jo has continually invested her personal touch. When I read her advice and use her products I feel like she's talking to me and that she really cares.

Barbara, UNITED KINGDOM

Shanghai Tang

Every time I slip on my favorite Shanghai Tang jacket I feel proud to be Chinese. Shanghai Tang is the embodiment of Chinese fashion heritage. Their clothes celebrate the art of the imperial tailors in every stitch and seam, and it brings a smile to my face when I think about our artistic heritage being given new life. Thank you Shanghai Tang!

Iris, HONG KONG

Toronto Maple Leafs

In a country where hockey is a religion and its arenas are its cathedrals, the Leafs are one of hockey's highest orders. This is a team you love or hate, but can't ignore. Leaf fans are loyal and will travel the world to support their team, and at home they have sold out every game for years. I am a Leaf fan and have never seen them win Lord Stanley's cup—yet I always believe.

Simon, CANADA

Vegemite

I lived in Australia for two years when I was 10 years old (I'm from the States and almost 40 now), and it was love at first bite. As this spread is an acquired taste, this marked me as an odd child. When we left Australia we made sure to take lots with us, and it was a sad day when the last jar was emptied years later. At the time it was almost impossible to find outside of Australia and New Zealand, and none of my American friends could understand why I missed it so....Of course now you can get Vegemite in the States easily, and, thanks to Men at Work, everyone's heard of it. But Vegemite remains special to me, a salty reminder of some of the best years of my life, the ones I lived Down Under.

Susan, UNITED STATES

Xbox

The full curve of the controller molds into your hands. The screen beckons, and you move through dark worlds. Your ears fill with the rush of rockets as you touch down on an alien landscape. Machine guns rattle on a historic battle ground. You immerse yourself in the intrigue of a strange, alternate reality. What could be more mysterious, sensual, and intimate than Xbox? Lovemark. No question.

Aidan, THE NETHERLANDS

California

When Saatchi & Saatchi offered a brand new Toyota Prius as the prize for the best nomination to lovemarks.com, Richard Vallens seized the opportunity. He wrote a great nomination for his Lovemark, Bike Friday, that you can read on the next page. Bike Friday is a small company that produces hand-built travel bicycles. I got to meet Richard in Los Angeles and present him with the Prius. What an amazing enthusiast—for Bike Friday, for the Prius, for life. And what a license plate. Here's Richard in full flight enthusing about his two Lovemarks, Bike Friday and the Toyota Prius. KR

The license plate on Richard Vallens' prize Toyota Prius.

DISCOVERING BIKE FRIDAY

My son and I have a long history of riding bikes together. At just five years of age, he rode 24 miles with me to the beach and back in one day!

As any parent knows, it's phenomenally important to listen as your child speaks. In order to do that it's important to be physically close to them. We felt we could never get close enough to chat well as we rode our single bikes, because you have to go single file. This all changed when I discovered the Bike Friday Family Tandem.

WHY BIKE FRIDAY IS A LOVEMARK

Nik and I got on our new Family Tandem for what I thought would be a trip around the block, a five-minute spin. We went out and my son insisted on going farther and farther. It was easily three hours before we got home on that bike.

I started that ride thinking, "I can't believe I spent this much money on a bike." By the time we got home, I was thinking, "I can't believe I got this much bike for that little money!"

What Bike Friday markets is enthusiasm, dreams of cycling in far-off places, and belonging to a worldwide community of owners. They sell precious moments with your kids and a way to be together as a family. Regular companies offer plain old bicycles; Bike Friday makes and markets dreams.

Ours has created such positive memories that it has achieved heirloom status, and will be passed down when my son has children of his own.

Bike Friday care about their customers. They have created a worldwide community of owners so, just about anywhere in the developed world, you can find people who have these bicycles, connect with them, and even go visit and ride with them. You'll end up with lifelong friends.

OWNING AND LOVING A PRIUS

I'm not sure I would have had the courage to choose a Prius as my new car, but it has turned out to be better than I could have ever imagined.

Dreaming

The Prius is eloquently engineered and has been thought through with remarkable care. Toyota hasn't missed the mark in a single area. I keep looking for the trade-off resulting from this car being a hybrid, and there just isn't any area in the design that's been shortchanged. It starts smoothly, drives smoothly, and stops smoothly. There's no downside.

The first week I had the Prius I let my neighbor drive it. A few days later he came to me and said, "Drive me to the dealership, I need to own one of these."

And he bought one! He drove it to work where a colleague saw it and said, "You know, I'd like to drive this car." Within three weeks my Prius was responsible for two more sales—and for good reason.

A Lovemark creates uncommon passion and loyalty among its users. I knew I had such a product after I bought my Bike Friday tandem bicycle. It's clear I have another in the Prius.

RICHARD VALLENS' WINNING NOMINATION FOR BIKE FRIDAY

My Bike Friday Family Tandem is a flying carpet of great magic, the perfect solution to the eternal quest of doing something with your kids where you can both have fun and truly communicate. My rides with my son (16 now, eight when we bought the bike) on our Family Tandem are the best, absolutely the best, memories he and I have. We've had a complete blast on this bike—physically close enough to talk and hear well (and conspire), with the bicycling effortlessly filling any gaps in conversation. I've learned everything about my son by being close enough to hear as his thoughts and impressions burble out during long Family Tandem rides. So many times, it was just us in our own world, father and son on the red bike. Bike Friday is my Lovemark.

Richard Vallens and son Nik with their Family Tandem Bike Friday in 1999.

Presenting Richard with his new Toyota Prius.

Defining that

Who can be surprised that Lovemarks instantly found a welcome home in France, the country where reason meets passion? In his book La Nouvelle Renaissance, *Philippe Lentschener, Saatchi & Saatchi's CEO for France, calls for society to find a new vitality by adopting wider values based around people. Here he beautifully articulates the emotional dimensions that motivate what we call Inspirational Consumers.* KR

A cultural model

For us, working in France, Lovemarks has acted as an anchor to what was already embedded as part of our culture. The elements of Lovemarks are second nature to the French, so our agency was immediately able to understand the power of emotion for both the brand and the consumer. Of course before Lovemarks we did not know how to encapsulate these feelings into an ideology. But now, in an incredible way, we are able to rationalize what is in fact psychological.

As a result, I think we are now at a point where Lovemarks have reached the status of being a cultural model. By that I mean that Lovemarks allow us to define ourselves through the brands we love.

Cultural experiences

The first brand that made this clear to me was the retailer FNAC, a company that is the European leader in the retailing of cultural products like CDs, books, records, and DVDs. This was the brand that first made me discover what a Lovemark really was and the power of Lovemarks.

Let me explain. In France the price of CDs and recorded music is fixed so there is no price competition amongst retailers. This meant that, when I went to buy a specific record I really wanted and found that FNAC was closed, I went to another store, a hypermarket. The thing is that as I left that store with the record in a branded bag I felt as though I had just made a utilitarian purchase. I realised that this was not how I would have felt if I had brought that exact same record from FNAC. When I've got a record and it is in a branded bag

'je ne sais quoi'

from FNAC I find I am proud to be in the street showing that FNAC is where I made my purchase. FNAC gives me an experience that the other stores do not. They make me feel that I am part of a cultural activity, and that experience makes them a Lovemark for me.

Defining yourself

To follow on from this, it is logical that, if a Lovemark is a cultural model that tells other people a lot about you, people will advocate for their Lovemarks. For example, if you are at dinner, you will naturally advocate for books and talk about books in a way that will also say a lot about who you are.

I have noticed that people who travel with easyJet in Europe are also great, great advocates of easyJet. Why? Because what they are in fact advocating is travel! They talk about all the possible destinations they would like to go to and then they tell you that they can afford all those destinations because of easyJet. It's a great experience going out to dinner with those sort of people and hearing their

enthusiasm because it allows them to travel so often. It makes you revisit the way you act, the way you participate, and the way you think.

The communication is so compelling because these people don't just advocate for their Lovemark, they advocate the environment of that Lovemark. It is through their enthusiasm for the possibilities of travel that they lead me to consider easyJet. That is indeed the power of a Lovemark. The experience of a Lovemark is always stronger than the details.

Certainly the Lovemarks experience has been quickly understood here in France. We have always had brands we loved but I don't think we had a very persuasive way of describing that. Lovemarks has helped us encapsulate this idea and put names to things we already knew in our hearts. It has been incredible.

Philippe Lentschener—
"Lovemarks allow us to define ourselves."

Tell someone about something you love— tomorrow.

Log off your computer. Handwrite five notes to people who matter to your business.

How do your favorite places in the world use Mystery, Sensuality, and Intimacy? Use these insights to transform your own town.

Make a list of well-known airlines. Invent some new names for them that open up fresh possibilities. Song titles are a great inspiration

Send a nomination to Loremarks.com. Tell a story that reveals how Mystery, Sensuality, and Intimacy made it your Lovemark.

CHAPTER FOUR

Creating Lovemarks

INSPIRATIONAL OWNERS

A 7-step guide to putting Lovemark principles into practice featuring comments from 27 Inspirational Owners, CEOs, and senior marketers. Included are AVEDA, Benetton, Ben & Jerry's, Camper, Dansko, Kiehl's, Montblanc, Segway, Silhouette, and Victorinox, manufacturers of the Swiss Army Knife.

Insight interview
Nicolas Mirzayantz, Senior Vice President, International Flavors and Fragrances Inc.

Love bites
Five things to do tomorrow

BEN & JERRY'S Ben & Jerry's Peace Pops entered my life during the first year of my second marriage. My husband and I each contributed three hyperactive, insecure, and demanding children. While we waded through that first year of trying to convince each little dear that we loved him or her to distraction, we occasionally slipped away to the local market for Cherry Garcia Frozen Yogurt Peace Pops. We sat in the car together and decompressed, reminding ourselves that we loved them and each other, and that we only had ten more years until the last one would be old enough to leave the nest! *Melanie, United States* • **HUFFER** I absolutely can't get enough of Huffer clothing. I started buying their clothing about six years ago; I have kept every piece I have ever brought, even if I don't wear it anymore! It's a connection between the clothing and me, like a friend. *Lucy, New Zealand* • **TUCK SCHOOL OF BUSINESS** How do I love Tuck? Let me count the many ways: there are approximately 500 of them in the classes of '05 and '06, and a bunch of them in faculty and staff positions. Put simply, in an age where people make the difference, those of the Tuck community rock. Tucked away in the bucolic backwoods of Hanover, New Hampshire, our school boasts the best and brightest of MBA talent, without an ounce of the arrogance or pretentiousness that you might find at other top b-schools. We make a difference and live life to the fullest in the process. *Leela, United States* • **SEGWAY** I look forward to my daily office commute because my Segway makes the two-mile trip sooo much fun. I now notice and enjoy the interesting things around town that used to just whiz by my environmentally-unfriendly car. I'm making friends with people who want to stop and talk about my wheels. The Segway is like an extension of my body, since it is so easy and intuitive to simply lean in the direction I want to go. It almost feels like when I have flying dreams. Just the sight of my Segway key, or the feel of it in my pocket, is enough to make me smile and rejoice: isn't life wonderful? *Rodney, United States* • **VICTORINOX** I love that little red shield and cross. My Swiss Army knife, watch, and travel gear are abiding reminders of things well-designed and well-made, a celebration of the pure joy that attends the meeting of beauty and utility. I like to have that unmistakable rich red color somewhere with me at all times. It's the color of quality, durability, efficiency, and self-reliance. *Tim, United States* **O'REILLY MEDIA** I look at the O'Reilly books lined up on the shelf in my office and feel like I can tackle any development problem the day might present. They're an encouraging, dependable partner. Whenever I google a problem, their online resource often appears on the first page of results. I love my support web. *Damien, New Zealand* • **DUMBO FEATHER** *Dumbo feather* is not just a magazine, but a labor of love. I'm so hooked: each issue is like a favorite pet that arrives in my mailbox on a regular basis. It's always read in one sitting the day it arrives, even if I'm propping my eyes open with matchsticks in the wee small hours. Once I've taken it all in, I carefully place it in a special spot with its sibling issues where guests to my home are allowed to look but not touch. Chances are the first person I let have a flick through will be the woman I marry. *Rory, Australia*

Stepping up to Lovemarks

Creating Lovemarks is all about the ability to understand consumers' dreams, to know what they want and when they want it, and to create great experiences that make your brand a loved part of their lives. This is the key to Lovemark success. Great Lovemarks come out of great passion—a commitment to creating long term emotional connections with consumers. A Lovemark will always be a great brand, but not all great brands are Lovemarks.

This chapter takes a step-by-step approach to how Lovemarks are created, from infusing brands with Mystery, Sensuality, and Intimacy to building sustained Lovemark communities.

To demonstrate how Lovemarks work in the real world we have illustrated each section with insights from top business leaders. These voices include Benetton's CEO Silvano Cassano, Ben & Jerry's CEO Walt Freese, Renzo Rosso, founder of Diesel, and Camper's founder Lorenzo Fluxa.

And what do these Lovemark stories tells us? That at the foundation of every Lovemark business is a commitment to putting the consumer's dreams for the brand ahead of everything else. As Lorenzo Fluxa of Camper says, "We base what we do on love and passion."

There is no blueprint for creating a Lovemark. Lovemarks stand out because they are personal and distinctive, not because they follow a set of rules. Your job is to make your own connections based on your own ideas, combined with the ability to inspire other people with these ideas. That's what differentiation is all about.

Shah Rukh Khan

Small ideas get buried fast. To win in today's market you have to live for big, emotionally connecting ideas. Big ideas with stopping power, with talking power. In the movie *The Player*, Hollywood mogul Griffin Mill only gives hopefuls 25 words to sum up their big idea. *Alien* was famously described in three words—"Jaws in space." How many words do you need?

The REAL world of business is anchored by Respect at one end and inspired by Love at the other. Propelling them both forward needs Emotion and Action. R-E-A-L. Respect, Emotion, Action, and Love: the essence of Lovemarks. KR

Bollywood superstar Shah Rukh Khan at the launch of Lovemarks, *Mumbai, India.*

1.

START WITH RESPECT

Businesses have analyzed and measured Respect for decades. But it keeps slipping through their fingers. The trouble is that consumers keep changing and the stakes keep going up. Respect has to be earned again and again, just as Love can only be given. Before you start out on the road to Lovemarks, you must have Respect. Too often I find businesses think of consumers as just another hurdle before making a sale. The first job then is to transform any consumer suspicion or indifference into Respect.

Here's the crunch question I have asked business leaders everywhere— is it better to be respected, or loved *and* respected? There's no contest. Everyone wants both.

Consumers themselves treat Love and Respect as indivisible. Try thinking of your favorite relative. Can you separate the emotions you have for them into neat Respect and Love boxes? Of course not. People forget that Respect itself carries emotional baggage.

Just as we did for Love, we have worked out the most important elements of Respect. Use it as a guide to action, not an excuse for more analysis.

PERFORMANCE	TRUST	REPUTATION
INNOVATION	RELIABILITY	LEADERSHIP
QUALITY	COMMITMENT	HONESTY
SERVICE	EASE	RESPONSIBILITY
IDENTITY	OPENNESS	EFFICACY
VALUE	SECURITY	

Take a long, hard look at the items on the list. Every one of them feels like a routine business expectation, until you wrap some personal emotion around it, and focus on your brand.

...comes around

Here are 12 tough questions on Respect. Give them your best shot. I can tell you that there isn't a business in the world that will not find some of them difficult to answer. Make sure you answer on behalf of your business and your brand. For a solid foundation of Respect you need to get an 80 percent pass rate.

1.
Does your brand perform better than your competitors do all of the time?

2.
Does your company always do the right thing by consumers? By the local community?

3.
Does your brand have a heritage that consumers know and care about?

4.
Are you sure your company is offering the best possible value?

5.
Do you get consistent feedback from consumers, and do you take it seriously?

6.
Do you have a put-it-right plan for when something goes wrong?

7.
Does your company welcome challenges to the way things are done?

8.
Does the way consumers perceive your brand match the reality?

9.
Would you recommend your brand to your best friend?

10.
Does your brand consistently deliver more than it promises?

11.
Is your brand the leader in its field?

12.
Does your company keep its promises, even if it might hurt the bottom line?

MANDARINA DUCK
First nominated by Maite,
SPAIN

"Our products respect the people who buy them in the sense that they're functional and fresh, they're worth the price, and they have a style that isn't imposing. This adds up to a sensation of what I'd call 'wellness.' That in turn creates a level of connection that is difficult to forget.

"We believe Respect can be the conduit for Love—Respect for colleagues, for clients, for all the people you connect with. The best way to show interest towards other people is do so with a duty of honesty and truth."

MATTEO ATTI,
BRAND MANAGER

2. GET CLOSE TO CONSUMERS

A fundamental of Lovemarks from the beginning was that "consumers own the brand." What does this mean? For a start, it requires every Lovemark business to be more interested in what consumers have to say to them, than what they want to say to their consumers. Sounds easy, but plays hard.

It's easy to surround consumers with your images and messages, but it's tough to connect with them. Here are five ways to get started.

ONE:
FORGET WHAT YOU THINK YOU KNOW

Every business is convinced it knows its consumers. But dig deeper. From what I can see, most of that knowledge can be found on a driver's license. You know where they live, but not how they live or who they live next to. You know their age, but have no idea about their dreams. You can know more about global CEOs from business magazines than most companies know about their own consumers. Make a commitment to do far better. Start asking them what keeps them awake at night, what they would do if they won the lottery, and how they celebrate good news.

TWO:
GET OUT OF THE OFFICE

When I talk about inviting consumers into the heart of your business, I'm not talking focus groups with pizzas and two-way mirrors. I'm talking genuine two-way conversations. Try talking to people on their own territory, not on yours. In their homes. At the store they regularly shop. And give them control. Let them set the agenda, decide on the menu, and write the rules. There might be time for the factory tour once you get to know one another.

THREE:
DON'T KEEP SECRETS

It's impossible to be invisible. Blogs are alert to every misstep. They have the power to amplify problems faster than any corporate communications department can control them. A Lovemarks relationship with consumers sets the same demanding standards as a love affair. Lie and you die.

FOUR:
SHARE THE PLEASURE, SUCK UP THE PAIN

People love to be part of a success. They want to feel that they made the right choice, whether it's the suburb they decided to live in or the shampoo they picked up at the store. They want their Lovemarks to be admired and emulated. Your side of the bargain is to keep the worries, problems, and hardships of your business to yourself. When things go wrong, fix them straight away. When you're in pain, don't share it with your consumers—suck it up.

FIVE:
LIVE THE LIFE

You can't understand consumers if you don't share their lives. That means shopping where they shop and playing where they play. If you run a hotel you need to sleep in every bed. If it's cars, try letting go of the wheel and taking a few trips in the back seat where the kids live.

BENETTON
Arousing emotions

"It's not always easy to find the recipe for love. The ingredients are many and always different for each individual."

I talked with Luciano Benetton, president of the Benetton Group, when I had the opportunity to work with students at the Benetton design school, Fabrica. Luciano was into Lovemarks and he is a great believer in the power of the individual to spread Love and make the world a better place. In his introduction to the Colors "Enemies" issue, Luciano wrote: "Conflicts aside, people want to live, buy and sell, fall in love. That which is divided by politics and religion is united by the daily, normal qualities of life and relationships."

This deep-seated belief in people has made Benetton a symbol of social and ethnic inclusiveness in many parts of the globe. Benetton and their famous advertising campaigns show how Mystery, Sensuality, and Intimacy can create long-lasting emotional connections with consumers around the world. Here's Benetton's CEO, Silvano Cassano. KR

"I believe that Benetton is a respected and well-loved brand because it has succeeded in setting up an actual exchange of ideas with consumers. Because this exchange has endured over the years, it continues to seek, express,

and arouse emotions. The men and women who love Benetton love it because they feel part of something, and because they know that something is part of them.

"It is not always easy to find the recipe for love. The ingredients are many and always different for each individual. They change in time and space. Tastes and passions change, just like the seasons.

"To help build this kind of relationship we always try to talk *with* rather than talk *to* our consumers. Likewise we have always tried to expand the context of our dialog. As you see from our way of operating, we always ascribe values to individual people rather than promote products or services at consumers.

"Identifying with an individual instead of a customer means that we can promote our company's products not on the basis of the age or income, but instead on a shared vision and a set of common values. It is consumer enthusiasm for this approach that explains why love given receives love in return.

"The Benetton story is one of passion. Our passion for colors, for young people, and for innovation."
Silvano Cassano

FROM LEFT: Carlo, Gilberto, Giuliana, and Luciano Benetton launched the Benetton Group in 1965. The Benetton family retains a majority shareholding. With its corporate headquarters located at Villa Minelli in Ponzano, Treviso, about 18 miles from Venice, the Benetton Group is active in 120 countries. The core business is clothing, including the casual United Colors of Benetton, fashion-leader Sisley, Playlife leisurewear, and Killer Loop streetwear. The Group produces around 110 million garments every year, has around 7,000 employees worldwide, a retail network of 5,000 stores, and generates a total annual turnover of approximately €1.7 billion.

BEN & JERRY'S
For the belly and soul

"We don't need everyone to like us, just some people to love us—passionately."

Ben & Jerry's is another business that understands that creating emotional connections through the application of Mystery, Sensuality, and Intimacy is the way to create vibrant businesses that consumers love. When I was young, ice cream came in vanilla and vanilla. Ben & Jerry's turned that model on its head and stuck an emotional flag in the ground for its consumers, as CEO Walt Freese explains. KR

"Ben & Jerry's is more than a product. It's a place, Vermont, representing simplicity; it's a branded company, willing to stand up for something in the world. We are also a reflection of the people who walk through our door every day.

"That's why our customers are Loyal Beyond Reason. It's because

we have brand personality—we are fun and irreverent—and we are authentic. And, of course, we offer amazing flavors that they can't get anywhere else.

"We also find that so many brands do not want to ruffle any feathers, they want to be liked, they're afraid to stand for something. Ben & Jerry's comes from a different place. We don't need everyone to like us, just *some* people to love us—passionately. And they are the ones that we take care of.

"That's why, when legislators in Washington, DC decided to open the National Wildlife Reserve in Alaska, Ben & Jerry's sent down employees and built the largest Baked Alaska in front of the Capitol. Greenpeace was associated with this action as well, in addition to a number of other associations. It was part of our broader fight against global warming. Ben & Jerry's takes a stand for just causes.

"Ben & Jerry's, at its essence, is about joy for the belly and soul. Everything we do comes from there." **Walt Freese**

George

GEORGE FM, NEW ZEALAND
First nominated by Dan, NEW ZEALAND

"Our listeners have an unceasing loyalty and passion for their station, and that's a responsibility that our station crew doesn't take lightly. Our listeners are Loyal Beyond Reason, I can't define why, but it's what makes our station great. It keeps us on our toes and always raising our benchmark.

"When a listener comes up to me and tells me how important George FM is in their life, and how it helps define who they are and what they do, it makes me humble and proud at the same time. I get a real sense that we are making a difference."

JEF KAY, STATION MANAGER

TUCK SCHOOL OF BUSINESS
First nominated by Leela, UNITED STATES

"Places of education are special and powerful far beyond their formal curriculum, and Tuck is an educational facility *par excellence*— challenging, personal, and beautiful. A gathering place where immensely talented students from all over the globe meet as strangers and quickly become an extended family.

"Tuck's alums are extremely loyal to the school. They quickly discover that the personal ties that form while earning an MBA at Tuck can blossom into a worldwide network of business colleagues and confidants that lasts a lifetime.

"In this very personal and challenging setting the students learn to love each other and, reinforced by a successful career, that love is transferred to long-term support for the school."

PAUL DANOS, DEAN

BENDON
First nominated by Karen, NEW ZEALAND

"Fashion is an industry that people fall in love with. All our communications aim to develop that emotional connection.

"The most significant experience I've had with Inspirational Consumers was when we sent out a survey asking for feedback about people's experiences of buying bras. Over one weekend we heard back from 1,500 people—many thanking us for a chance to involve themselves in the process of designing a bra and our willingness to listen."

STEFAN PRESTON, CEO

SILHOUETTE
Listening beyond reason

It's not hard to see how family businesses are quick to understand the power of Lovemarks. When we developed the Lovemarks qualities we used the family as a model of how Love worked as the emotional connection between people. Arnold Schmied is president of Silhouette US, the family-owned global eyewear company based in Linz, Austria. Arnold has taken Lovemarks and applied it in the highly competitive world of eyewear. It is a business that combines well-being with fashion, a tricky juggling act that Lovemark companies thrive upon. Here is Arnold speaking of his combined passion for eyewear and Lovemarks. It's a great combination, as you will see. KR

"There is so much to learn from brands that aspire to be Lovemarks, especially if they are sincere in trying to bring value, excellence, and passion to consumers who, most of the time, think that they have seen it all.

"When I became aware of Lovemarks we followed in the footsteps of lovemarks.com and developed our own website for consumer stories about our top product—Titan Minimal Art. Within a couple of months we collected close to 3,000 beautiful stories at silhouettestories.com, all of which make it clear that people do have a loving relationship with our eyewear. We really did not expect this!

"As a prize we invited six consumers and six eyecare professionals to visit our parent company in Austria for an Austrian experience. All these stories have contributed strongly to strengthening the Mystery around Silhouette.

"Another new experience was being approached by a very good optical account of ours with a business idea. I invited this group of opticians first to our home office in the US and then to our parent company in Austria. In brief they had successfully expanded sales of one of our rimless products from adults to children. Inspired by their story we developed—with their input—our first real children's collection. This was a first for us—and all because of listening beyond reason." **Arnold Schmied**

Silhouette International is a family-owned business that employs more than 1,600 people. Arnold and Anneliese Schmied started the company in 1964 with the intention of "transforming eyewear from a visual aid into a fashionable accessory." Beginning with a staff of five, the company now has 13 distribution subsidiaries, including the United States, Germany, United Kingdom, Norway, Sweden, Denmark, Italy, France, Spain, and Japan. In all, thanks to its distribution partners, Silhouette is represented in more than 100 countries worldwide.

The company has combined its efforts to create attractive eyewear with a strong interest in technical development. Its hingeless Titan Minimal Art frames are now used by all NASA astronauts. Silhouette produces all its own eyewear in a process that retains a high level of handcraft with only 20 percent automated processing.

Silhouette produces 2.3 million pairs of eyewear annually under the Silhouette brand and an additional 1 million pairs of eyewear under licence for adidas and Daniel Swarovski.

"There is
so much to
learn from
brands that
aspire to be
Lovemarks..."

ARNOLD SCHMIED

3. FIND OUT WHERE YOU STAND

There are many different paths to becoming a Lovemark. Here are two Lovemark tools that can start you on the Lovemark adventure or act as insight generators to help you keep your Lovemark alive and well.

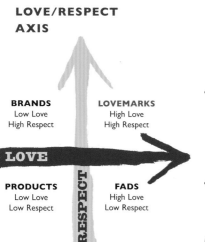

LOVE/RESPECT AXIS

BRANDS
Low Love
High Respect

LOVEMARKS
High Love
High Respect

LOVE

PRODUCTS
Low Love
Low Respect

FADS
High Love
Low Respect

RESPECT

ONE: LOCATE

- Work through the Lovemarks elements and locate your brand on the Love/Respect Axis. It might help to separate the company from the brand, and be clear about whose point of view you are taking. Usually it will be the consumer's perspective, but you may want to check out investors or partners and see what differences this makes.

- If you're into metrics you can use the Axis to award points for each Love and Respect quality, average them out, and use the result to plot your position.

- Use the Lovemarker to get a sense of where you are strong and where work needs to be done.

Using the Lovemarker

- Scoring: 2 points for Hot, 1 point for Warm, 0 points for Cold.

- No Respect, no Lovemark: You must score at least 25 Respect points to be considered for Lovemark status.

- What your points mean:
  0 to 36 points—commodity
  37 to 40 points—brand
  41+ points—Lovemark!

TWO: GENERATE

- Where would consumers put your brand on the Love/Respect Axis?

- Discuss the difference between the perception of your brands and business compared to your own thinking about your positioning. Go through the Lovemark qualities and test each one for ways to bring perceptions and reality closer together.

- Discuss how you can apply the Lovemark qualities to your brands or business to take you from your current position to the Lovemarks quadrant on the Axis.

- Come up with at least five insights and convert them into action plans for people to take away and get started on.

THREE: COMPETE

- You know where your brand sits on the Love/Respect Axis. Now locate your top five competitors.

- Work through the Lovemarker elements and decide where your competitors have out-Lovemarked you.

- Come up with 50 ideas that can help close the gap. Develop five of them.

- Leave the whiteboard behind and unleash your ideas in the marketplace.

FOUR: STRETCH

- Use your inside knowledge of your industry. Select four brands, one for each quadrant of the Love/Respect Axis.

- Develop specific, actionable strategies for how each brand could become a Lovemark.

- Focus on the differences in what is required to get out of the fad quadrant, the commodity zone, and the brand corner.

- Go to lovemarks.com and put your brand through the Lovemark Profiler.

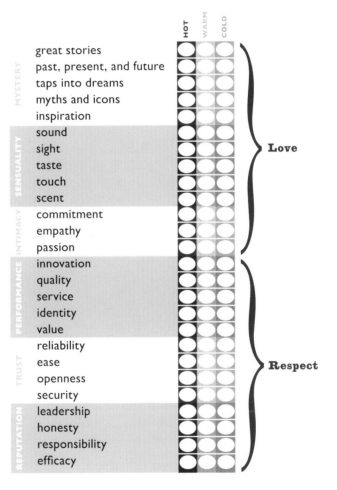

THE LOVEMARKER

		HOT	WARM	COLD
MYSTERY	great stories	●		
	past, present, and future	●		
	taps into dreams	●		
	myths and icons	●		
	inspiration	●		
SENSUALITY	sound	●		
	sight	●		
	taste	●		
	touch	●		
	scent	●		
INTIMACY	commitment	●		
	empathy	●		
	passion	●		
PERFORMANCE	innovation	●		
	quality	●		
	service	●		
	identity	●		
	value	●		
TRUST	reliability	●		
	ease	●		
	openness	●		
	security	●		
REPUTATION	leadership	●		
	honesty	●		
	responsibility	●		
	efficacy	●		

Love

Respect

DUMBO FEATHER With integrity, love, and passion

"From the outset I said that if Dumbo feather inspired just one person to follow their dreams, I would have achieved mine."

When Kate Bezar, editor and founder of Dumbo feather, asked me for an interview, I was pumped. This is just the sort of magazine I love—opinionated, feisty, and totally in tune with its readers.

Kate calls Dumbo feather a "mook," a magazine and book. There you go: and/and showing its power again. Here she recalls how she aimed this award-winning publication toward the top right hand quadrant of the Love/Respect axis. KR

"I was trawling the web for ideas to help me develop the brand for the publication and stumbled on lovemarks.com. The framework immediately struck a chord—it encapsulated all the ideas and notions I'd had floating around in my head in a succinct, pragmatic way.

"Every single aspect of Dumbo feather—be it the design, the website, or any other touch-point—reinforces what it is. That it is real and authentic and made with integrity, love, and passion. Readers sense that and are loyal because of it.

"From the outset I said that if Dumbo feather inspired just one person to follow their dreams, I would have achieved mine. When readers email me to tell me how Dumbo feather has inspired and impacted their lives, it means everything to me.

"We're often asked where the name comes from. It's not explained anywhere—not in the publication itself, not on the website, nowhere. Some people get it immediately, while others have to google 'Dumbo feather' to figure it out. But once they have, they feel like they're in a club of those who know. Mystery leads to curiosity, curiosity leads to inside knowledge, and inside knowledge leads to a sense of belonging." *Kate Bezar*

CAKEWALK
Realizing musical dreams

With their SONAR software Cakewalk inspires their customers and helps them recapture their creativity. They have done this by keeping their eyes firmly on the Love quadrant of the Love/Respect Axis. Marketing Director Carl Jacobson tells the story. KR

"The CEO of Cakewalk, Greg Hendershott, handed me the Lovemarks book and said there were many concepts that we could apply to our marketing activities. It confirmed many things that he had instinctively felt about our success, our brands, and our relationships with customers.

"I try to apply the concepts to what we do, especially by thinking of ways to further enhance our relationship with our customers. The Love/Respect Axis is like a compass for our activities, always pointing northeast—we hold it up to our plans to see if we are headed in the right direction.

"Ten years ago you would have needed tens of thousands of dollars and access to a professional studio to do what SONAR allows you to do at home. I get constant feedback from our customers that they have been empowered by what we do.

"We use elements of sight and touch in our packaging. On our new Project5 box we used different gloss finishes. Beyond giving alternate light reflection, each finish has a different feel, so when someone picks up the package, they have a tactile experience. A sense of detachment often comes with the experience of making electronic music, but with Project5 the packaging ensures that the software is as inspiring and touch-sensitive as a real instrument.

"In the end though, consumers love Cakewalk products because they enable them to realize their musical dreams." *Carl Jacobson*

Carl using Cakewalk's SONAR 5 software.

"The Love/ Respect Axis is like a compass for our activities, always pointing northeast."

4. TRANSFORM WITH MYSTERY

Drowning people in information is a major turn-off. People love to be intrigued and to make discoveries for themselves. Why else are "secret formulas" so successful? Why else do we hang out for the surprise ending?

ONE:
UNDERSTAND THE POWER OF STORIES

Every brand has a story, and the best ones often come from consumers. Identify the key elements of a great story—character, setting, conflict, plot, style, and so on. This is an important way to begin to understand why some stories are more powerful than others out there. Collect every story you can find about your brand and then go out and ask consumers for any stories they have. You will be amazed at the insights these stories will open up for you.

You may need an experienced storyteller to get you moving in the right direction but the bottom line is that these are *your* stories.

People can tell what's authentic and what's not in a heartbeat. The potential is huge to begin to tell your stories in innovative and exciting ways. Camper provides the story of its origins with every pair of shoes it sells. People love this connection of the past with the present. It makes them feel part of the Camper story.

TWO:
GET INTO ICONS

Great icons have always worked hard to bring a sense of Mystery to brands. The Pillsbury Doughboy with his charming giggle has delighted generations of consumers. Agree on the 10 most famous icons in the world, and then invent one of your own. It won't be easy, but there's no better way to get insight into the essence of your business. You will find icons work when they connect with emotional truths. That's a long way from a corporate graphic that no one can remember.

THREE:
BECOME DREAM MERCHANTS

Once you are not at the center laying down the law, there is room for consumers to participate. We know that every brand means something a little different to every consumer. Love lies in these differences, and one of the most dynamic differences is dreams. By getting in touch with what consumers dream about, you can reveal profound insights into their needs and aspirations. How you get to those dreams is less important than what you do with them. Shoppers could have dreamt forever about somehow taking a relaxing break in the supermarket. This was all fantasy until some supermarkets responded by opening coffee shops in their stores.

LONELY PLANET

First nominated by Margarita,
UNITED STATES

"Recently someone said *Lonely Planet* is about the 'oh wow' and the 'dammit!' moments. That sums it up pretty well.

"'Oh wow' when the guidebook tells you about this amazing rock art and rocky plateau at Ubirr in Kadau National Park—so amazing that you almost have to sit down to absorb it all. And 'dammit!' when you're suddenly lost in a strange place on a cold, wet, dark night where you can't speak the language and your trusty guidebook helps you find that warm and safe bed!

"What makes *Lonely Planet* special for so many people? It helps them be brave, it helps them take the journey that they might not otherwise take, and it helps them connect with the world."

JUDY SLATYER, CEO

Lonely Planet *cover image—young Aboriginal dancer from Cape York Peninsula, Australia.*

CAMPER Looking out on the mountains of Majorca

People love shoes. Many of them have shoes as their Lovemarks—and some great companies have been created on the soles of the world's feet. In the story of shoes Camper has a special place. I think their company catchphrase "walk don't run" says a lot. Slow down and enjoy what you experience. This spirit has taken Camper from a small Spanish island to the world. Here founder Lorenzo Fluxa reveals the heart of Camper. KR

"Being from the Mediterranean is the source of our authenticity. The rural atmosphere, history, culture, and landscape all influence Camper's aesthetic and values. I would say that if good solid values have been the foundation that has kept us on the right track, the dream and the passion are what has kept the fire lit through the years.

"Our way of understanding freedom and respecting personal identity is to apply creativity in a spontaneous way. We group our products by concepts—some evolve over time in almost imperceptible ways and others change more frequently, exploring new, surprising routes.

"We like to evaluate Camper not only by profits but also by how we invest our profits and how we follow good business ethics. For example our Wabi shoe respects the natural shape of the foot and also respects the environment. The three components—shoe, insole, and sock—can be separated and independently recycled. The materials used are 100 percent recyclable and the insole is bio-degradable.

"Most of all we base what we do on love and passion. We have a mind-set that we share with our customers. We don't impose it, we share it. We enjoy making our shoes and we feel lucky and blessed that we have a following of Camper fans." *Lorenzo Fluxa*

Camper was founded on the island of Majorca in 1975 by Lorenzo Fluxa using the skills of generations of local shoemakers. The name Camper is Catalan for "peasant"—early designs were modeled on peasant footwear. In 2004 Camper sales topped €135 million with more than 3 million pairs sold worldwide.

"...the dream and the passion are what has kept the fire lit through the years."

Artistic Twins, a Camper shoe where the design starts on one foot and continues on the other. Art by Pep Rossellò, a Majorcan painter.

SEGWAY HT From innovation to everyday use

When you see a Segway in action you have to put it at the top of the list for Mystery. Most people know that the Segway® Human Transporter (HT) was the result of years of intensive research and development. Segway's inventor, Dean Kamen, came up with the idea after seeing a young man in a wheelchair struggling to get over a curb. He realized that the problem wasn't ineffective wheelchairs; it was the fact that the world was designed for people who could balance. Once this assumption is challenged, a whole range of innovative product ideas are free to be explored.

Klee Kleber, Vice President of Marketing at Segway LLC, points to the connection between the Segway and Lovemarks. KR

"Riding a Segway HT is so intuitive it becomes one with the rider. This leads to what we call the inevitable "Segway smile" and an emotional connection that makes it a Lovemark.

"The launch of the Segway HT was a mysterious story. In fact, an entire book was written to chronicle this Mystery and the work of the people who brought the product to market, including, most importantly, Dean Kamen.

"Even now new product development, which happens behind closed doors, creates an environment of speculation and Mystery among the enthusiast customers, with technical and product topics debated at length in online chats that our employees and executives also take part in.

"We are lucky in that there are few products that are as social in nature as the Segway HT. Our customers are constantly stopped by other people and asked about the product, so there is ample opportunity to advocate and demonstrate loyalty. In fact, within one year since the Segway HT went on sale to the public, an enthusiastic community of Segway HT owners had formed."
Klee Kleber

> **"Riding a Segway HT is so intuitive it becomes one with the rider."**

5. TRANSFORM WITH SENSUALITY

Human beings live through their five senses. They are the rich context that allow us to choose between the things we love and those we avoid.

ONE:
TURN UP THE MUSIC

List the songs that come closest to the relationship you want with consumers. Don't just take lyrics into account. Pace, tone, rhythm, and volume all make music distinctive. I remember Microsoft astonished the world by using the Rolling Stones' hit *Start Me Up* to launch Windows '95. What a big emotional promise! If they had kept that passion alive they could have become one of the most loved companies in the world. Today any brand can open the ears of consumers. Just make sure it's about them, not you. You want to entertain them, not put more marketing mash into their bowls.

TWO:
EMBRACE SCREENS

The hard, reflective screen is usually regarded as the opposite to the sensuality of Lovemarks. Your challenge is simple then: reinvent Sensuality so it includes the screen senses. After all, the screen is

the marketplace for this century. Screens play to our senses of sight and sound every day. Not only has the mobile phone elevated touch, deep in laboratories around the world scientists are working to capture taste and smell. Get there first. Ask the youngest people in your business how screens touch their senses. Believe them.

THREE:
ASK FOR A HAND

From designing cars to designing shoes, consumers are doing it for themselves. To them it's customization. To you it can be inspiration. Sensuality means getting physical. Don't just ask a few questions and filter out the answers you don't like. Get people to play with your product, let them get their hands into the packaging and encourage them to make prototypes that work for them, no matter how weird they seem to you. Their first attempts might look like Frankenstein's monster, but if there is the germ of an idea in there, their hybrid will be a thing of beauty. Never forget consumers are smart—that's why they buy your brand.

FOUR:
GET IN TOUCH

Beware of blandness. The brands that offer new sensual experiences will become leaders. Start simply. When you print business cards, add texture to the paper. Try embossing to leave a touch memory in anyone who holds one. Test all your packaging with texture in mind. Live with your products. A small but perfect change can make a product sing without adding cost.

FIVE:
DON'T GET HUNG UP ON TASTE

A lot of people find the sense of taste a challenge. If they are not in the food business they figure it is irrelevant to them. Use taste as a surefire way to stretch your brain. Imagine you manufacture bricks. You might not want to eat one, but bricks don't have to be tasteless. Start with a beautifully-built wall with the caption "the sweet taste of success." Consider sponsoring a fine food award or creating chocolates that look like bricks. The perfume creator Demeter have scents called Grass and Vinyl. I'm sure brick would be a breeze!

AVEDA
Loving the moment

"I'm not interested in competing, I'm interested in making a contribution. If someone else is doing organic, I consider them a colleague."

If you ever doubted the power of Love as a business practice, you haven't listened to Horst Rechelbacher, founder of AVEDA and Intelligent Nutrients. His profound understanding of the power of Love permeates everything AVEDA does. They were the first company to sign the CERES principles for corporate environmental responsibility in 1989. Horst, who now heads Intelligent Nutrients, regards his commitment to sustainability as his calling. KR

"Love is my therapy. Loving the moment is where information meets chemical matter. When we love, our body releases chemical compounds known as endorphins that interact with neuropeptides and boost our immunity.

"The first sensory connection with a product, next to aesthetics, is always through aromatics.

AVEDA aromatics provoke stimulation and relaxation, and they bring pure, fresh nature into the moment. The sense of smell, like all the other senses, is directly linked to our memories and emotions. This is a valuable lesson for Lovemarks.

"We are identifying what we want when we smell it, see it, hear it, touch it, feel it, taste it. In other words, we all identify our needs through our sensory system, which also determines what we desire.

"That's why AVEDA's network of beauty and healthcare professionals service their clients with love and care. The interactive experience with our products is a love-creating factor. It is about human kindness, and this is linked to intelligent business.

"Love has no boundaries. I have always been devoted to creating a company where this is part of the mission statement, and where sustainability is linked to products and consumer relationships.

"I'm not interested in competing, I'm interested in making a contribution. If someone else is doing organic, I consider them a colleague." ***Horst Rechelbacher***

Tablet **Hotels**.com
Unique Hotels for Global Nomads

TABLET HOTELS
First nominated by Jane,
UNITED STATES

"What makes our clients loyal to
Tablet Hotels? We have integrity.
We are our own worst critics.
We work hard and it shows. It is
not just about looking good or
feeling good. There are few things
more disappointing than being
physically attracted to someone
and then finding out that you
cannot really talk to this person.
Substance is what makes people
loyal. We look good and you can
talk to us!

"For us, it is sometimes a fine
line between persistence and
stubbornness, optimism and
delusion. While we believe that
our clients are loyal for good
reasons, we go beyond reason
to make it work."

LAURENT VERNHES, CEO

FRITOLAY
First nominated by Gregory,
UNITED STATES

"Working in the snack world,
taste is something that we try
to communicate as an emotional
experience rather than a physical
attribute. It´s what brings people
over and over again to our brand—
not just any brand that could copy
our taste.

"Once a consumer was talking
about how our brands were part
of their family. They welcomed the
brands into their home every day.
I realized that Lovemarks become
part of families and thus need to
behave as such."

ALVARO SANCHEZ,
MARKETING DIRECTOR,
FRITOLAY COLOMBIA

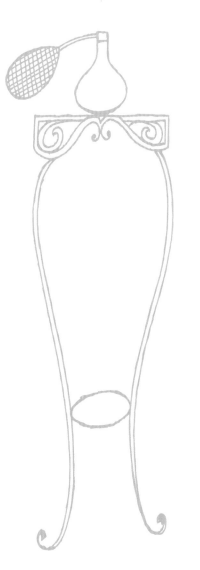

scents and

International Flavors & Fragrances Inc. (IFF) has been producing taste sensations and scents to covet since 1833. When I met Nicolas Mirzayantz, I knew straight away that he completely understood the power of the senses. I asked him to share with me his passion for exploring the magic and Mystery of scent. KR

Creating scents as Lovemarks

For many years now we have been urging the market to recognize the importance of making emotional connections with consumers. The idea of creating Lovemarks, brands which resonate emotionally with consumers, is at the very heart of IFF's creative work.

Scent is a key ingredient in creating a Lovemark. It embodies Intimacy, Sensuality, and Mystery. It creates the most intimate connections with people because it remains on skin, clothes, children, and lovers.

Sensuality too is implicit in fragrance. Scents are known to arouse, to be aphrodisiacs. Think of musk, ylang ylang, or patchouli. These are all very sensual scents. There is also Mystery. When you meet somebody their perfume can create fantasies, stimulate memories, and alter perceptions about them.

Arousing emotion

Flavors and fragrances are powerful triggers of desires, aspirations, and dreams. In developing fragrances it is critical to create passion by tapping into these powerful human desires. It can bring us back to the basics, our primal instincts. Take memories for example—scent has the power to recreate things that have long since gone.

One of my favorite treasures is an old leather bag that my grandfather owned. Every time I open the zipper I can smell him. It's like a genie— open the bag and my grandfather appears. That smell transports me back to some of the happiest times of my life.

Smell is probably one of our most powerful senses, but we often just use our noses to breathe. In February 2005, IFF partnered with the Museum

sensibility

of Art and Design in Hamburg to educate people about the world of fragrances. The exhibition *Perfume: The Aesthetics of Seduction* was created to enhance people's understanding of the emotional power of scent.

The science of emotion

IFF has been working to understand the connection between emotions and scents for nearly 20 years. One of the most important insights we have discovered is that fragrances can actually be engineered to produce specific feelings and moods. We can examine the emotional connection a fragrance makes with a consumer, and whether that connection is appropriate for a specific brand.

When we ask people to smell our scents we ask them, "How do you feel?" rather than, "Do you like it or not?" Instead of fragrances that everyone will like, we create fragrances that certain people will love. Fragrances they will be loyal to for a long time. We are able to engineer the passion factor into a fragrance, something that is vital to the brand's long-term success.

Our research shows that when a scent has strong emotional resonance rather than just high hedonic acceptance it is more likely to succeed than when it does not have that emotional connection. It is the brands that have the strongest emotional resonance that are the most successful.

The aroma of colors

People often think about the senses as having just one function—the nose for smelling, eyes for seeing, and ears for hearing. They don't often think about how interrelated the senses are.

Our sensory science department has created a mood-mapping protocol that has led us to understand how fragrances evoke moods, colors, and textures in consumers' minds.

One of our most important successes in innovative scents in this field was Polo Blue by Ralph Lauren. Ralph Lauren Fragrances asked us to develop a fragrance which could evoke a particular shade of blue in the minds of the consumers. We were able to enhance the blue profile of the scent by

Nicolas Mirzayantz—*sensualist, creator of fine fragrances, and emotional connector.*

including very specific ingredients. If you ask people what color comes to their mind when they smell the scent blind, they will come up with one of four related shades of blue.

We also ask people to smell some of our ingredients and to "feel" certain textures. We ask them, "Which of the different textures comes closest to the way you perceive that scent?" In this way we are able to develop a multi-sensorial profile which includes specific feelings and moods.

Emotion versus function

More and more consumers today seem to be seeking experiences and emotional benefits rather than product attributes and functional benefits. In every single category around the world we are talking about emotion, we are talking about experiences.

At IFF we believe that while the functional benefits of many products are table stakes, it is the fragrances or the flavor that will add value and bring the consumer to loving the product. But no matter how much you love a brand, no matter how much you love a concept, the advertising, the packaging, the positioning, at the end of the day if you don't connect emotionally with the scent or the taste you are less likely to come back and buy it again.

Innovation

We're constantly reaching out to people who are thinkers, who are trying to break the boundaries, to reach new frontiers and new territories.

We worked with the art editor at *Visionaire* on two issues, focused on scent and taste, respectively. Most of the time perfumers are asked to create under constraints because of quantitative hedonics, test results, brand visions, or other factors. Rarely are they given the opportunity to express their true creative vision as artists. It was wonderful to give carte blanche to our perfumers to create scents for the publication. For *Visionaire: Scent*, our perfumers developed fragrances for concepts not traditionally associated with a scent, such as mother, cold, noise, electricity, and hunger.

Visionaire: Taste is a groundbreaking collaboration that combines the scientific and creative talents of the world's leading flavorists, contemporary artists, chefs, and photographers. We've created works of art that stretch the sensual boundaries of the imagination by simultaneously engaging the viewer's eyes and tongue. Featured concepts are luxury, orgasm, art, and guilty, to name a few. This is one of the greatest projects we have ever worked on.

There are so many territories we have not explored and we're constantly getting new ingredients and creating new scents. If you look at music—which has only seven notes—how many new melodies can you create? We have thousands of ingredients. Can you imagine the infinite combinations that are possible? There are so many possibilities, yet sometimes the market is just not ready for them.

We see our role as a guide in the olfactory world, forever inspiring people to expand their scent vocabulary and experience life through the nose. It's a powerful place, where anything is possible.

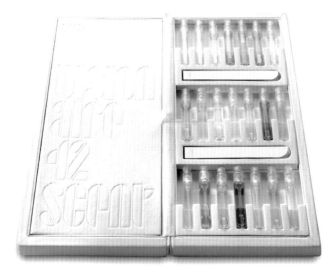

Visionaire: Scent, *Issue 42, 2004.*

6. TRANSFORM WITH INTIMACY

The sensitivity that Intimacy demands of us means that of the three elements of Lovemarks, Intimacy responds fastest to change. Take the mobile phone. What used to be the symbol of hard-charging business has become the closest companion of millions. This transformation alone shows the passion people have for emotional connection.

ONE:
TAKE ACTION

One phrase to strike from your vocabulary is, "I hear what you say." Hearing is one thing, but doing is another. How about taking a deep breath and saying, "I'm going to act on what you just said." Too often priceless consumer insights sit forgotten on someone's desk or hard drive until they are archived, then trashed. I remember a client showing me a stack of forms. They were from a survey done two years before, but never analyzed. I looked at the top sheet and there in careful handwriting was the comment, "You need to take more notice of your customers." The key to Intimacy? Listen, listen, listen, and act.

TWO:
BUILD IN LAYERS

Intimacy and Mystery have many connections. The special sense of belonging that Intimacy brings is created by revelation, not explanation. Explore your brand to find resonances consumers can uncover. It could be a thoughtful comfort like a luminescent drink holder for night driving or a bench in exactly the right place in the store.

THREE:
REMEMBER BIRTHDAYS

Relax. I'm not talking about printed messages in corporate greeting cards. Remember the times when a gift touched the sweet spot and fired up unforced enthusiasm? How does this happen? It's simple. The perfect gift is all about the person who receives it, and it's all about you at the same time. It is a great emotional connection tied up with a ribbon. Your consumers can't love what you produce unless they can see you love it too.

FOUR:
LEARN TO LET GO

Customization is the pragmatic face of Intimacy. The bar has certainly been raised in a world where people can customize anything from their sneakers to their automobiles. The big question to keep asking is: where can consumers get more involved? People like to participate when they have meaningful choices. The father who shows a son how to paint a wall but never hands over the paintbrush is missing the point.

FIVE:
GET INSPIRED BY FAMILY

Love is two-way. Forget this and people drift away. Use the idea of family as an inspiration in your business. Identify the stories and language that show why your organization needs to do what it does, rather than what must be achieved. Sharing is the foundation of family. Sharing is how you create a family that is emotional, proud, and fiercely loyal. Sharing is the essence of Intimacy.

TIFFANY & Co.

First nominated by Pamela,
AUSTRALIA

"The Tiffany's customer feels proprietorial and often calls the company 'my Tiffany's.' To many, it was the Tiffany's of their parents, grandparents, and great-grandparents.

"They each have fondly remembered experiences and cherished family heirlooms. Tiffany's is part of their family. Many go so far as to name their daughters Tiffany. That is Loyal Beyond Reason and a claim no other brand name could make.

"Our customers are loyal to us because we, in return, are loyal too—steadfast in our commitment to offering them only the highest quality."

JOHN LORING,
DESIGN DIRECTOR

Audrey Hepburn as Holly Golightly in Breakfast at Tiffany's, 1961.

VICTORINOX® SWISS ARMY™ KNIFE

"Our passion is human understanding. Our art is beautiful function."

The Swiss Army™ Knife is a global icon. More than that, it carries another Lovemark on its bright red side panel, the internationally loved white cross on the red of the Swiss flag. Like many people, I have owned a number of Swiss Army™ Knives and have used them to open impossibly taped packages and remove the cork from bottles of wine. There is nothing more intimate than exploring the various blades and functions on a Swiss Army™ Knife. Anyone who owns one knows the delight at discovering the stainless steel tooth pick and watching the delicate maneuvering of the small scissors as they set back into their place. The Swiss Army™ Knife is a powerful tool that has embraced intimacy as a key element of its brand. We were delighted to hear from Carl Elsener, a direct descendant of the knife's creator. KR

"The key connections we make with the Swiss Army™ Knife are trust, promises kept, sentimentality with the association of the knife as a rite of passage, and delight in uncovering the functionality and ingenuity.

"We believe that the tradition of giving or receiving your very first pocket knife pulls past, present, and future together. When our brand loyalists see the cross and shield emblem on our other, newer products, the Mystery is immediately there.

"In terms of Sensuality you just need to hold a Swiss Army™ Knife in your hand to experience the shape and texture and to explore each of the implements. In terms of Intimacy we hope that our products reflect the commitment, passion, and empathy that have always been a part of our heritage. Honesty, integrity, passion, and ingenuity are Victorinox's guiding principles, from product development to marketing. Our passion is human understanding. Our art is beautiful function. This will always be our goal.

"We understand that brand loyalty comes from winning both the hearts and minds of our consumers. We also understand their special relationship with the Swiss Army™ Knife and the expectations this experience creates for our brand. This has made us extremely disciplined in how we go about developing new product lines as we build our brand globally.

"Every product in all of our additional product lines (watches, travel gear, apparel) needs to reflect the attributes and values of the Swiss Army™ Knife and deliver on the expectations that it has created among our consumers. The more we understood the passionate following created by the pocket knife, the more important maintaining and inspiring this same relationship became as we undertook new endeavors. We think this focus on the passionate relationship that existed with our consumers has allowed us—and is the only thing that will continue to allow us—to be successful with our expansion into new product lines and markets around the world.

"As we say in our brand statement, 'We believe it is not enough to provide raw function and utility.' Those values alone don't satisfy the heart. It is beautiful design that brings our products to life and continues to inspire the extraordinary brand loyalty of our most passionate consumers. Our knives are born of human hands and minds for human needs. They have a heart and intelligence. They are made like you." **Carl Elsener**

Karl Elsener created the Victorinox® Original Swiss Army™ Knife in 1897. The well-known cross and shield emblem was added to the knife in 1909. Today approximately 25,000 Swiss Army™ Knives in 100 different models are produced daily by 1,000 employees. Victorinox also produces 30,000 pocket tools in 300 different models along with 45,000 household and professional knives a day. Ninety percent of these products are exported to over 100 countries.

The name Victorinox is in memory of founder Karl Elsener's mother Victoria, while inox is the international designation for stainless steel.

Carl Elsener, CEO of Victorinox and a direct descendant of the creator of the Swiss Army™ Knife.

DANSKO Driven by our customers' love

"We've heard from brides who wore their Danskos down the aisle, from nurses who routinely work 18 hours straight in theirs."

Local, global: Lovemark ideas can come from anywhere, that's the beauty of them. Amanda Cabot and Peter Kjellerup changed from running a successful equestrian business in Pennsylvania, USA to selling clogs they had discovered on a horse-buying trip to Denmark! Amanda shows her faith in the power of a Lovemark community when she talks about how important the response from consumers is to the brand and the business. KR

"Instead of having growth as our goal, we aim for a positive emotional response from everyone we deal with. Our business model is simple: we are driven by our customers' love for us.

"We're not just in the shoe business, we're in the life business. We believe passion shows through a company's communication. When that passion includes a commitment to improving the quality of life for anyone, we're intrigued.

"One way we define loyalty is the willingness to spend time writing or calling in response to the unsolicited messages we receive daily from our business associates and consumers. In turn we hear back from consumers. We've heard from brides who wore their Danskos down the aisle, from nurses who routinely work 18 hours straight in theirs, and from athletes who can't wait to put on their Danskos after skiing or running or biking. These encounters help us maintain the integrity of what we make and how we sell it.

"Our stated mission is to be our customers' favorite—not the only shoe in our customers' closets, or the only brand on our retailers' shelves—but their favorite. There's nothing in Dansko's mission about being the world's best or largest; in fact, there's hardly anything quantitative about us. On the contrary, we foreground the qualitative experience.

"And our employees? Well, how could we possibly fulfill our mission without being their favorite company, their Lovemark, as well? It's the trust, loyalty, and commitment of all these links that ensures our success. This is simple and self-fulfilling." *Amanda Cabot*

MONTBLANC
An intimate accessory

For all the wonders of new technology, I still prefer to use a Montblanc when I write. There is something about the physical link between hand, heart, and brain that attracts me, along with the personal nature of handwritten notes. You will see by their comments that Montblanc's managing directors, Wolff Heinrichsdorff and Lutz Bethge, really understand the power of intimacy and what is important in life. Here they touch on so many qualities we have identified as important to Lovemarks. KR

"The act of handwriting is very closely linked to Love and Respect. We have all experienced that in an age where you get 100 emails a day, taking the time to write a letter or a note by hand signifies more than the pure exchange of information.

"I have always found that a handwritten letter is perceived as an individual gift, a gesture of appreciation, warmth, intimacy, and love. So, while every typewriter and every PC can be named a writing instrument, it is only the writing instrument that fits into the hand that really develops a close relationship with its owner. This also explains why a Montblanc is often handed down

from generation to generation, an intimate accessory in people's lives." *Wolff Heinrichsdorff*

"For me writing with a Montblanc is about taking time for the essential things in life, things that really matter, like friendship, trust, love, and gratitude. When a Montblanc product first enters the hands of its owner it already has a fascinating story to tell—a story of traditional European craftsmanship, the pride and passion of a master craftsman, and the cultural values it embodies. From there the owners surround their Montblancs with their own stories." *Lutz Bethge*

"For me writing with a Montblanc is about taking time for the essential things in life..."

7.

CREATE A LOVEMARKS COMMUNITY

A Lovemark is only as good as the people who love it. That's why Lovemark companies attract communities. If you can prove to consumers that you care about their well-being, their future, and their relationship with the brand, they will reward you with Loyalty Beyond Reason. With the right combination of Mystery, Sensuality, and Intimacy, you can create a connection between people who are scattered throughout the world. A community of consumers who all feel part of a family with shared experiences.

In the contributions by CEOs of Lovemark companies you will find some fantastic ideas to help you start your own Lovemark community—from Fluevog encouraging consumers to help in the design of their shoes, to Remo's infectious website where consumers revel in the ability to take control and have fun at the same time.

3M POST-IT® NOTES
First nominated by Andre, SOUTH AFRICA

"To be a loved brand means attracting loyalty—the dream of every marketer. The brand is in the consumer's eyes and there's an emotional connection.

"When Post-it® Notes were launched they changed the office environment. Now they have more than one important role in our end-users' lives. They allow people to be in touch with others—mothers sending notes in their children's lunch boxes, spouses leaving notes in suitcases when their husband or wife travels, messages on bathroom mirrors."

M. JEANNINE CURRIE, COMMUNICATIONS MANAGER, 3M OFFICE SUPPLIES DIVISION

LUSH
First nominated by Veronica, ITALY

"Sometimes our products will start merely as words suggested by customers that inspire us to make products to match. How do I know? Because I often take part in our web-based customer forums. We have a fanzine called *Lush Times* and fans who call themselves Lushies. I attribute this level of loyalty to the fact that we wear our heart on our sleeve.

"My thoughts on what makes us a Lovemark are best captured by ten words: Provocative, Honest, Fresh, Innovative, Fair, Great Products, Safe, Fun, Teasing."

MARK CONSTANTINE, MANAGING DIRECTOR

O'REILLY MEDIA
First nominated by Damien,
NEW ZEALAND

"Our customers can tell, from the way we think and write about technology, that we care about the same things they do. At our best we give voice to our community.

"We convene summits and working groups, bringing together tech influencers and even our competitors to wrestle with the big issues facing us all. We even spearheaded a public protest against one of our biggest retailers when they engaged in business practices that threatened the technology community. Not obvious business moves, but effective ways to learn from our customers, represent them, and nurture the bond we share."

TIM O'REILLY, FOUNDER

EVIAN
First nominated by Bonita,
UNITED KINGDOM

"A Lovemark is not just a brand people love, but also a brand that loves people: answering their needs, making their life easier, fitting their way of life, acting for their well-being.

"Recognized as a 'source of youth,' Evian believes youth is not a question of age, but of attitude: with Evian, keeping body and mind 'young and healthy' is within everyone's reach!"

THOMAS KUNZ,
EXECUTIVE VICE
PRESIDENT BEVERAGES,
GROUPE DANONE

HUFFER
First nominated by Charles,
AUSTRALIA

"My attitude is that life is a beautiful thing and being in business is a raw exercise. You learn a lot about yourself and the world around you. I love the idea of starting with nothing and making something.

"Everyone has something valuable to say, so listening intently is part of it. Mostly we try and please ourselves and our buddies and let the direction and the identity take their own shape."

DAN BUCKLEY, FOUNDER

KIEHL'S
Beyond a brand

If you are looking for a textbook demonstration of putting Lovemarks in action, Kiehl's is a prime contender. This remarkable company has been creating skin and hair products for 150 years. CEO Philip Clough is very clear about what makes Kiehl's a Lovemark. KR

"From our earliest years we have formulated products in direct response to customers' requests, and while we are a bit more sophisticated about formulas today, everything we create—from products to the overall in-store experience—has the individual at heart.

"We observe traditions and time-honored values, one of which is to treat customers as friends and extended family. We believe in attentive, personalized interactions and environments that foster conversation. It's a part of who we are as a company—nearly innate, certainly intuitive—and it's what creates our visual and emotional fabric.

"We've rewarded devotion through the Kiehl's bus tour. We visit our customers where they live and work and distribute gifts of their favorite formulas. The bus tour has always been about celebrating both our most loyal customers and unsung heroes in the community—a mobile event that we've taken to sanitation workers for keeping the neighborhood clean, post office workers for delivering rain or shine, animal hospitals for keeping pets healthy, and firemen and -women for keeping us safe.

"Beyond being a brand, we're guided by the idea that one of the purposes of our existence is to improve the quality of the community in some way and to share our passion. That's what makes us a Lovemark—we express our passion and we support projects that are important to our customers. We learn from them and we get the opportunity to be educators ourselves."
Philip Clough

> "...one of the purposes of our existence is to improve the quality of the community in some way and to share our passion."

GIBSON GUITAR CORP

First nominated by Tim,
UNITED STATES

"Gibson is a lifestyle; it's about entertainment and bringing a piece of your soul to your audience, be it an audience of one or an audience of 20,000.

"The essence of Gibson Guitars is in the people who play them. It is the spirit and the emotions that are tied to the product that make each and every one an integral part of the owner's life."

HENRY JUSKIEWICZ,
CHAIRMAN AND CEO

REMO General Store
The community is the brand

Remo Giuffré has always had a natural affinity with his customers and a passion for the new. It's not surprising that REMO is now an online store with a large community of Inspirational Consumers in all parts of the world. Remo demonstrates how to create Lovemarks networks and keep them entertained, in touch, and inspired. KR

"When the REMO General Store opened in Oxford Street, Sydney in 1988, it's not as if I had a customer-based model in mind. We found that a store that manifested my personal passions and those of a coterie of friends attracted smart customers who had similar values. And they had ideas. 'You're stocking this, why don't you stock that?' or, 'You've done that T-shirt design, why don't you do this one?' Because I'm a consultative person by nature, it evolved into this community. It was only when I started working with companies in the US that I understood what it was and why it was so successful in engendering, in Lovemark terms, this Loyalty Beyond Reason.

"Because we involved our customers in the development of our offerings, we broke down the wall that traditionally exists between a brand and the customer. We said, 'Wait a minute, we're all customers. It's not them and us. Them equals us.' What we're saying is that the community is the brand. The bottom line is this: a customer network is the most valuable asset that any brand can lay claim to. I feel that over time most of the smart retailers will get wise to the benefits of a more networked approach where customer involvement is core.

"We read and listen to every comment. In the pre-Internet days of course it was a lot harder, but we did the best we could. We had suggestion boxes in the store, we had catalogs in which we asked, 'Your feedback please. What do you like? What don't you like? What are you thinking, we'd love to know.' Many aspects of REMO, lots of our best ideas, have come from our customers. Ideas for our café, new product development ideas, improvements to our existing merchandise. Most of our product development ideas can probably be traced back to a suggestion from a customer.

"Sometimes a customer has an idea for a T-shirt design. Often I've just broadcast to a subgroup of customers who are flagged as designers and said, 'So and so from Madison, Wisconsin thinks that the pyramid with its "all-seeing eye" on a United States greenback would look great on the front of a T-shirt. Does anyone want to do this?' And a couple of designers come back, 'Yes, I've got a bit of free time, I'll do it.'

"Old habits die hard, especially the model of, 'We're the brand, you're the customer, shut up and consume. We'll let you know.' To pull down the curtain that separates the back office and the front of the store, you've just got to hold your breath and do it.

"I do believe that it's the right thing to do. At the street level, you can see micro examples of it. For example, restaurants where you can see everybody making the meals. I saw a restaurant in Santa Monica where not only was the kitchen visible from the street, but the refrigerated room too. You could see people walking in and grabbing the slab of raw meat. You've got to have a pretty tidy operation for that to work. But transparency is exciting for people, and involvement in the process has always been exciting for customers."
Remo Giuffré

"We said, 'Wait a minute, we're all customers. It's not them and us. Them equals us.'"

Remo Giuffré—merchant extraordinaire, brand owner, strategist, and creative director.

Look backwards. Draw from your history. Even a short past is a rich source for creating a distinctive identity.

Raise the bar. Collect stories in newspapers or magazines about consumers who inspire you. Circulate them to everyone in your business.

Make it real. Events and experiences make fantastic, lasting connections with consumers. Invest your time, energy, and love in them.

Get in touch with people who connect with your brand. Listen intently to what they have to say. Then do something about it.

Find your Inspirational Consumers. Invent ways to keep them curious, excited, and inspired about what you do.

CHAPTER FIVE

Romancing the shopper

LOVEMARKS IN-STORE

The next creative revolution is unfolding—in-store. An investigation into attracting the shopper with Mystery, Sensuality, and Intimacy.

Insight interview
John Fleming, Chief Marketing Officer, Wal-Mart

Special feature
Andy Murray, CEO, Saatchi & Saatchi X

Love bites
Through the eyes of the shopper
Payless, Costa Rica
Five things to do tomorrow

THE BODY SHOP
Think of the no animal testing promise, the fighting for noble causes, and the preservation of our world through their diverse programs to educate and reach out to individuals. I'll stamp a Lovemark on my Body Shop goodies basket! *Sara, United Arab Emirates •* **OLAY** The brand grew with me without losing its familiarity. When glass bottles broke, they created a plastic one. During adolescence they were right there with an oil-free brand. When melanoma became a concern in my 30s they were there with SPF. It's been 28 years of daily usage now and you'll never see me going for botox! *Maria, United States •* **LIVING NATURE** Living Nature is fantastic for its product, price, and ethics as a provincial New Zealand business supporting the local community. It is going from strength to strength without compromising its original principles. *Rebecca, New Zealand •* **KIEHL'S** Kiehl's shower products were the first non-brand producer of quality body care products, since imitated by hundreds, still the best and true to original principles. Simple, pure, and effective. They make me squeaky clean, soft-skinned, and sweet-smelling every morning. *Barry, Australia •* **LUSH** Soap goes veg. Pink like a candy bar and delicious like a coconut in a midsummer night. Lush smells like a warm pillow that listens to my dreams while I am sleeping. Lush is a tender bath that always covers me with joy. *Veronica, Italy •* **BOOTS** In England when you're sick—do you go to the doctor?! Nooo! You go to Boots…because there's something about the staff in their pristine white uniforms that makes you feel like they know what they're talking about…and actually seem to care. Sure, there are other similar shops that are cheaper…but they're just not Boots. *Sarah, Germany •* **KING OF SHAVES** Until I discovered King of Shaves products, shaving was torture for me. Now I can shave twice a day if necessary without the merest hint of a rash. Heartfelt thanks to the guys and gals at King of Shaves. *Mike, United Kingdom •* **AVENE** Pureness of the lines, pureness of the smell, pureness of the texture, pureness of my skin after using the products…this brand is totally pure and I love that, beyond reason. *Audrey, United States •* **MAC** I am absolutely in love with MAC's lipglass! The variety of colors and finishes is amazing, the texture is perfect—not tacky, and the smell and taste of it is so familiar and comforting. I would be absolutely devastated if MAC ever took lipglass away from me. *June, Singapore •* **AVEDA** Aveda is more than a product or a way of life, it is a family of professionals that are passionate about this industry and all people and their well-being. I am honored to be a part of that family and what it brings to this world. *Sherry, United States*

Taking care of myself

The Theater of Dreams

Television may have been the greatest selling medium ever invented, but watch out—the next creative revolution will take place in-store. I believe the store will be the center of opportunity for businesses around the world, but only if they change the consumer experience. To make real emotional connections in-store we will need to turn them from functional machines into Theaters of Dreams. From stores to stories.

Lovemarks move the focus onto consumers and what they want. A great way to start the relationship is to ask, "Who is shopping?" The answer is women. Women make more than 80 percent of the buying decisions in all homes. Now manufacturers and retailers are starting to take notice of the power of female shoppers. We need to get used to putting women at the center of our shopper conversations. We need to be more personal—start to substitute "he" and "him," with "she" and "her." Sure, it might sound a little strange to begin with, but it is amazing how quickly you get used to it.

Our research in the United States shows that a typical shopper takes 21 minutes to do her shopping—from the time she climbs out of her car until she gets back in with her purchases. In those 21 minutes she buys on average 18 of the 30,000 to 40,000 products available to her. How does she do it? You can bet it's not by rational evaluation of every choice.

We now know that emotion, intuition, long-term memories, and the unconscious make up as much as 85 percent of our motivations. This means the store is full of potential for Lovemarks. In 2004 we embraced this potential and created the Saatchi & Saatchi X network, a specialist shopper marketing business.

In this chapter John Fleming, Wal-Mart's Chief Marketing Officer, gives us an insider's view of how the world's biggest retailer is about to transform its business through customer insights. We also have Andy Murray, Global CEO of Saatchi & Saatchi X, challenging us to look through the eyes of the shopper and see the store as she does. Also check out the key tools developed by Saatchi & Saatchi X to turn shoppers into buyers. Jorge Oller of Tribu/Nazca Saatchi & Saatchi in Costa Rica is a passionate supporter of Lovemarks. Jorge tells us here how Mystery, Sensuality, and Intimacy have transformed his client Payless from a price-focused store into an experience loved by every woman who goes through its doors. KR

Launch of the Lovemarks *book, Paris, France.*

The Merchants of

When I imagine Lovemarks in-store, I think of a world that's all about the life of the shopper. Both celebrated and contentious, Wal-Mart clearly knows a lot more about shopping than low prices. With 130 million shoppers in their American stores every week, and almost 50 years in business, Wal-Mart has a unique perspective. Chief Marketing Officer John Fleming is building on Wal-Mart's phenomenal logistical enterprise with customer insights. His goal is nothing less than to reinvent the Wal-Mart experience for millions of shoppers. KR

THE CHANGING WORLD OF WAL-MART

Our focus on low prices has proved to be very, very effective. When you consider that Target and Wal-Mart started in the same year, and then you compare Target's $50 billion and Wal-Mart's $312 billion in sales last year, you can see customers want what we offer.... the price thing works! People everywhere love low prices.

In the early days people who lived in small towns and rural communities had an incredible emotional attachment to Wal-Mart. We brought choice into the lives of millions of people. We gave them access to a huge range of products that helped make their lives better, as well as outstanding value through our always-low prices.

Once we asked some customers, "Where's the Target around here?" And they said, "Let's see, there's a Target down Highway 7 about five miles..." Then we asked, "Where's the Wal-Mart?" And they said, "My Wal-Mart is…" For them to personalize like this is an emotional thing. This is the connection that has made Wal-Mart successful.

We are now opening stores in places that already have every world-class retailer. Access to products is not in question. We are talking about shoppers who can choose where to buy and who are prepared to pay more to have the right experience. The question is, what if we can give them an experience they really like, even love, and also save them money? This is where we need to go.

We want to transition the deep emotional attachment we have with the heartland of America to connect with urban consumers. If we can do this

Bentonville

in the right environment, with the right assortment and low prices, they're going to feel smart about shopping at Wal-Mart. We haven't made that leap yet, but that's where we're going.

PLANO, TEXAS

Our new store in Plano, Texas has been an amazing advance for us. Plano got headlined over and over in the media as "Wal-Mart's going upscale," but upscale doesn't tell the story about why this store is important.

In Plano we wanted to get smart about what sets the tone, and then tune what we offer these customers. Retail, by and large, is won and lost locally. Only 3,000 products are different in Plano from our usual stores—that's 3,000 out 130,000. We've been able to tune our selection of wines, for example, to local tastes. Customization changes how people think about Wal-Mart. To be universally useful. And locally relevant.

Language can set the tone. On the front of the store it used to say "Food Center." We changed that to "Market." Where we said "Entrance," we now say "Welcome." Simple and obvious perhaps, but so much warmer.

We made big changes to the store layout based on customer insights. Retailers used to try to "get 'em in and keep 'em in" as long as they could. Historically we had put food on the opposite side of the store to health and beauty aids, but at Plano we brought them together. This change has had a powerful effect on shoppers because what they are looking for is a convenient and enjoyable experience.

Customers told us that the stores were too cluttered, they couldn't tell where they were going and we didn't have the right products next to each other. All this we could fix. We had always used the aisles as selling space but at Plano we gave them back to customers. We took product out so customers could move through the store more easily. Now they spend less time searching and more time shopping.

A better shopping experience is just part of it. It's the assortment and the experience, together with the breadth of products. That's what differentiates us. No one has the range of products we have—from iPods

John Fleming—*creating theater in-store for Wal-Mart.*

> ## AS A MERCHANT I HAVE ALWAYS KNOWN WHAT CUSTOMERS THOUGHT OF WHAT WE OFFERED IN STORE. WHAT I DIDN'T KNOW WAS WHAT THEY MIGHT BE LOOKING FOR.
>
> JOHN FLEMING

to oranges, tires to socks, swing-sets to lipstick. When I came to Wal-Mart six years ago I thought we had way too much stuff. Now I've come to learn there is magic in the number of categories that we carry.

The beauty of being a retailer is that we're not married to any particular product. Retailing is all about finding customers and keeping them satisfied by giving them access to whatever they need.

UNDERSTANDING SHOPPERS

The amazing thing I learned from Wal-Mart's online channels was what customers were looking for and didn't buy! As a merchant I have always known what customers thought of what we offered in-store. What I didn't know was what they might be looking for. Online gave me this view.

There are basically three ways customers shop us. First, they shop us frequently and they buy lots of categories. Second, they shop us frequently but buy limited categories. Third, only in an emergency. The names we have for these shoppers are Loyalists, Selectives, and Skeptics.

I think the Loyalists love us. Their lives are better because they can do all their shopping in one place. We've thought about their complete household needs and wants. We're convenient. They trust our pricing.

For the Selective Shopper, it's a transactional relationship. We need to understand her better and to ask, "Where do we meet her needs, what are the gaps, how can we ignite a positive emotional connection with her, what will it take?" I'm talking about changing the environment, getting much more disciplined in how we develop the assortments by category, and making it much easier for her to shop.

WAL-MART'S JOURNEY

We are definitely on a journey. We need to connect the dots on the price, the experience, the product assortment, and the community. And we need to spend more time to create the theater and the excitement of what retailing has always been.

Our operational efficiencies allow people to get what they need, but we have to work across the whole spectrum of what we can do for people to have a better life. Our unique size and scope give us a fantastic opportunity to make this happen.

Sustainability is where we can make a big contribution. We have the world's largest private truck fleet. In the next three years we will reduce energy consumption in that fleet by 25 percent, and by 50 percent in the next seven years. We are also looking to radically reduce our amount of waste. As a test, one of the toy buyers was given the challenge to make all the packaging as tight and light as possible. Just the first program meant 3,000 fewer containers were needed to freight the toys. By following sustainable principles we can actually reduce costs.

Organic products are another huge opportunity because our research shows this is something many of our customers really care about. Organic products are still very expensive, but by committing to long-term contracts with farmers we can support the conversion of fields to organic crops. We have done this with cotton suppliers in Turkey so we can launch baby clothing that is organic cotton and only 10 percent more expensive than regular cotton.

THINK LIKE A MARKETER, ACT LIKE A MERCHANT

For 20 years I was a merchant. Generally, merchants are very product-focused and are rewarded on their ability to find product and sell it better than their competitors. They are fast, intuitive, and very, very tenacious. Great merchants understand who their customers are, but they don't spend a lot of time thinking about them. By contrast, marketers think a lot about customers. They ask tons of questions because as it can take a couple of years to develop a new product, they have to get the right answer. Marketers are more analytic than merchants.

At Wal-Mart most of our merchants are focused on selling the supply instead of creating demand. I think there is an opportunity to create a new model. To think like a marketer and act like a merchant.

The new look Wal-Mart, Plano, Texas.

The retail revolution

I want to show how Lovemarks thinking can be used in-store. In the most recent edition of Lovemarks: the future beyond brands *I added a new chapter devoted entirely to shopping. That's how important I think this opportunity is for all of us. I have seen global companies concentrating considerable attention on how they can get closer to shoppers and make their in-store experience more enjoyable. Andy Murray's discussion of the dramatic changes faced by retail is supported by a suite of concepts and tools developed at Saatchi & Saatchi X. These take us behind the scenes and give us insight into how Lovemarks can work in-store, and with a little imagination, shape the shopping experience.* KR

Stepping up to the challenge

The retail industry is changing dramatically with the convergence of economic pressures, technological innovation, and the explosion of choice. We are seeing a true revolution in how we shop, where we shop, and when we shop.

Consumers' expectations of shopping have changed the rules. On the web consumers can now compare prices, personalize the choices they are offered by their purchase history, get any information they need with a click or two, and arrange to have it delivered where and when they want it.

Every retailer is asking the same question: what will the future look like? And then, of course, what it will take for us to get there faster? My question is different. Who will be the courageous few to bring imagination to the shopping experience? Retailing should not be confined by the store, but inspired by the shopper.

The focus of Saatchi & Saatchi X is to turn shoppers into buyers. We work across the total consumer environment, find insights into a shopper's behavior, and understand what creates Intimacy, Mystery, and Sensuality.

Andy Murray—turning shoppers into buyers with Lovemarks.

Through the eyes of the shopper I

SHOPPING EXPERIENCE FRAMEWORK

Shopping is a seamless experience. For shoppers it doesn't start at the door of the store, or end at the check-out. It starts at home and ends at home, and each shopping experience feeds into the next.

Saatchi & Saatchi X have identified 12 key activity points that form a framework for any shopping experience. Whether the shopper is in a supermarket, a mall, a boutique, or a sports stadium, this framework structures the experience consistently. And because it focuses on the experience from the shopper's point of view, it generates valuable insights into her choices, needs, and desires.

BEFORESHOPPING
PREPARATION

PROMPTING
"What does that remind me of?"

ASSESSING
"I wonder whether I need to shop today?"

LISTING
"What exactly do I need?"

PLANNING
"Where is the best place for me to shop today?"

WHILE SHOPPING
SELECTION

ARRIVING
"Is this the right store for what I want?"

SEARCHING / DISCOVERING
"Where do they keep the items I want to look at?"

EVALUATING
"Is this the right one for me?"

SELECTING
"Is this the one I want?"

PURCHASING
"Can I buy this one?"

AFTER SHOPPING
EVALUATION

ASSESSING THE EXPERIENCE
"Will I go back there?"

UNPACKING
"Did I get everything I needed?"

STOCKING
"Did I get enough?"

CONSUMING
"Is this as good as they say?"

ASSESSING
"Will I buy this again?"

> **Whatever their size, too many retailers take their customers' feelings, aspirations, and preferences for granted.**
>
> ANDY MURRAY

Turning shoppers into buyers is a much bigger idea than just what's happening in the store. We have to start the engagement with shoppers much earlier, before they set out to shop. Then we can move with them through the shopper cycle of planning, searching, and selecting, until they make their choice.

Virtually every major marketer and retailer is investing in research as they struggle to understand shopping and shoppers better. Already they have warehouses full of data and computer files loaded with transaction history. Unfortunately, this kind of information has not only become the bare minimum you need to be in the game, it doesn't even guarantee success. Eighty percent of new products and services either fail or fall short of their profit forecast in the first year. We still find it difficult to understand how a consumer will respond to new brands or retail ideas.

Responding to the revolution

The opportunity to thrive in the retail revolution lies in understanding what shoppers really experience in the store. Step inside and the senses should come alive as we are absorbed by smells, sounds, and things to touch, see, and taste.

As the price gap across retail formats closes and competition increases, the ability to create exciting and relevant shopping experiences becomes a key differentiator. It takes rich imagination to work in the three-dimensional, highly contextual world of the store. With over a million places to shop in North America, for example, the potential seems limitless—but today many of those places share the same aspiration. From Rodeo Drive fashion boutiques to clearance malls, retailers know they must transform the shopping experience.

Take the 138,000 convenience stores in North America. They are adding gourmet coffee and food items. Even fresh fruit and perishables are starting to show up. This is really exciting in a business that has traditionally been about gas, cigarettes, and beer.

Grocery outlets aren't sitting still either. Today 60 percent of all shopping trips are for five items or less. The stock-up trip is dead. Mass market grocery is responding by looking more like a convenience store. Some are putting in cafes so they can attract people who need to purchase lunch. They are building on the well-known fact that at 3 o'clock in the afternoon 70 percent of women in North America do not know what they'll have for dinner that night. The reasoning is simple. If they are having lunch in a café at the grocery store, they may also shop there for dinner.

The clear trend is for people to shop in more places and at a more times. Businesses are beginning to respond. Take movie theaters. When the old idea of "dinner and a movie" was sideswiped by home theater systems and DVDs, movie chains struggled to maintain their appeal to many audiences. One of the most successful responses has been based on reinventing their retail experience.

The Loews chain is doing a great job by offering a combined restaurant and movie experience. It makes sense. After all, the cinema is already a retail space where you go to buy entertainment.

The potential of shopping

Although cutting-edge retail spaces like Whole Foods and Best Buy get a great deal of media coverage, the potential of everyday shopping is just beginning to be tapped. There's a tremendous amount to do. The truth is that most store environments lack imagination.

Retail is such a transaction-driven industry that everything is about this hour, this day, this week. It's hard for people to take time out for imagination. Retailers have more data than dreams.

Whatever their size, too many retailers take their customers' feelings, aspirations, and preferences for granted. It's one thing to say they are the center of everything you do, and another to live by that claim. Retailers are busy with practical concerns like staying in stock, pricing, and transaction flow. Few of them develop a deep understanding of their consumers as people.

Through the eyes of the shopper II

SHOPPING'S EMOTIONAL DRIVERS

To find out why women like shopping we turned to psychology and anthropology. First we asked a psychologist to interview women who shop across a range of environments. They responded to questions asking why they like shopping, and what kind of emotions were evoked by different types of shopping and across different types of stores and categories.

Next we called on an anthropologist, who we asked to shop with women and bring back observations of how they responded to different kinds of stores and shopping experiences. We also asked the anthropologist to undertake intensive cultural interviews, to find the similarities and differences in the shopping experiences of women from different cultural backgrounds.

This analysis is the result of these findings—a fascinating insight into the way women shop.

SECURITY

"Being a good shopper means I can give my family a better standard of living."

She understands that her shopping is critical to the well-being of her family and those she loves and cares for.

SOCIAL RANKING

"Shopping for the right things at the right store makes me feel good about who I am."

She embraces shopping as a social statement and understands how this influences where she shops.

SELF-CREATION

"The things I buy help define who I am."

She sees shopping as one of the ways she defines herself. As someone once said, "People don't buy brands, they join them."

DREAMING

"There is more to shopping than just listing what I need."

She likes to imagine all the possibilities that are available in-store as she shops.

PLAY

".... and it's fun."

She delights in shopping as a fun activity.

ADVENTURE

"Shopping is such an adventure, it plays to my strong sense of curiosity."

She has a strong feeling of being "in the know" and enjoys shopping as a form of treasure hunting.

LEARNING AND MASTERY

"There is more to shopping than most people think."

She knows that shopping is an acquired skill like any other.

TIME-OUT

"Shopping is a welcome diversion in my life..."

She enjoys the ability to use shopping as "time-out" from her regular daily routine.

CONNECTION

"Shopping brings me in contact with other people in my community."

She thinks of shopping as a time for social connections both within the store and through the things she buys.

Emotion in-store

You can't get to reason until you go through emotion—that's a fact of brain function. Most of what you see in the store is being filtered in the visual cortex of the brain, which is the emotional seat. Unless what you experience passes through emotion, it's not even going to reach logical decision-making.

That's the problem. Too many stores see themselves as a place to demonstrate functional benefits. This doesn't make much sense. For a start, our eye-tracking research shows that shoppers only notice 50 percent of what they look at, even standing in front of a shelf. This is especially true in the critical first two-and-a-half seconds. If you don't catch their eye and their attention in a way that's emotionally and aesthetically compelling, the moment is gone in a flash.

The power of imagination

Insights are signposts. They point the way, but they don't describe the destination. The powerful step to take is the next one—from insight to foresight. To ask, "Where is this place going to go in the next two to three years?" and "What part can we play in that evolution?"

Foresight gets you to the dream. This isn't going to happen by itself. To create a Theater of Dreams, you have to look to the future with imagination.

This is very different from insight, which builds in increments from what you're already doing. Insights are often useful in validating the dream, but they are seldom of use in creating it.

Einstein summed it up when he said, "Imagination is more important than knowledge."

Through the eyes of the shopper III.

30ft
DELIGHT
Sound, Color, Motion
Mystery

10ft
DISCOVER
Engage, Brand
Intimacy

3ft
DECIDE
Touch, Scent, Taste
Sensuality

SHOPPER ATTENTION ZONES

There are three attention zones all shoppers pass through as they approach a purchasing decision. The first job for in-store design is to use a combination of sound, color, scent, and motion to attract attention from a distance—the 30 foot zone. A different approach is needed at 10 feet where placement on the shelf and the ability of the brand to stand out from its competitors is at stake. At three feet the consumer is either holding or reaching for her potential choice. It is the look, feel, and design of the object that will turn her from shopper to buyer.

Three keys to winning in the retail revolution

1

Packaging that works within the creation of the in-store environment.

Designing appealing packaging that shoppers actually see demands an intimate knowledge of shopping. The package has to work on the shelf, do a better job of informing the shopper why a product is unique, and must explain how the product works. This combination can only be achieved by skilled people with insight and imagination. The context of the shop has to be recognized as being critical to package design from the very beginning of the design process.

2

Retail environments that connect at all three layers of shopper communications—navigation, inspiration, and information.

Our research shows that the only concerted effort to communicate goes on navigation—routing people through the store—how shoppers spend only 6 percent of their time in-store. To attract attention requires delighting the shopper at all stages of the shopping process. Music, lighting, inspirational design, demonstrations, taste tests, and events. Imagine the impact of inspiring communications, touch-screen guides, and consumer-friendly entertainment centers in-store!

3

Technology that puts shoppers in control.

Retailers have largely relegated technology to the back office, except for self-checkout and pay-at-the-pump. Technologies that can put consumers in control have the ability to transform the shopping experience very rapidly. An excellent example is the mobile phone. With over 1.5 billion mobile phone subscribers, the possibilities they open to retailers are enormous.

For all the talk of in-store TV and the power of retail as another media channel, perhaps the digital future will not only be played out on screens on shelves, but on screens on shoppers. Shoppers can use their mobile phones to compare prices, find recipes, watch film clips, or check the precise ingredients in a product. The consumer will control the technology, not the other way round. They will choose whether or not they engage, and the winners will be the stores that use the technology to give consumers an inspiring screen-based experience.

Through the eyes of the shopper IV.

SHOPPER PASSPORT

Our research showed us that many executives working in the shopper arena were not shoppers themselves! Often too busy during the week and otherwise occupied in weekends, some of the executives we spoke to struggled to name the price of a bottle of milk and had only shopped occasionally during the year. How could we make busy business executives really understand shopping? We invented a role-playing tool created to challenge clients to experience shopping as consumers do. We called it Passport.

We supplied our "shopper" with a passport outlining the profile of a typical consumer, and included a shopping list and a budget. On their way to the store we threw in a Chance Card that introduced an unexpected everyday challenge: a reduction to this week's shopping budget or maybe an unexpected guest requiring more food on the same budget.

We then let let them loose in a real store to find, select, and purchase the items on their list. Along the way they have to make the trade-offs every shopper knows about, between what they need and what they can afford.

With Passport's role-play, clients don't simply observe or read a report, they participate in real time. We have found that people doing the Passport exercise are surprised at the personal insights it brings into every aspect of the shopping experience.

Through the eyes of the shopper V

DREAM STATE

Right now most store environments lack imagination. Retailers and marketers have got more data than dreams and we need to change that.

We work by starting with what we call the Dream State. With clients we identify what the ideal shopping experience is—no barriers, no bars, just a Dream State where you ideally see from the shopper's perspective. And then we design it and it becomes a vision for how this space should really be shopped.

It's very challenging to get people to use their imagination for how shopping could be more mysterious, more intimate, and more exciting as an experience.

Sample Dream State for a dog food display.

MORE LOVE

I vividly remember Jorge Oller, President of our Costa Rica agency Tribu/Nazca Saatchi & Saatchi, arriving at the first Lovemarks conference in New Zealand in 2002—he was carting bottles of his Lovemark hot sauce, Salsa Lizano. If Jorge was a believer in Lovemarks when he arrived, he pumped up the passion another 100 degrees on his return home. Jorge has described this transformation to me as changing from "piranha to dolphin." The agency's clients are now joining them on their Lovemarks adventure. Here's Jorge to take up the story. KR

I came back from New Zealand ignited by a simple idea. As a result we changed the name of our shop from Consumer (a word with no meaning in Spanish) to Tribu (the word for tribe in Spanish). We did it because we realized we needed to build a new relationship—we had to stop targeting consumers and start thinking of them as people.

Everything we've done, even the design of our new building and our offices, has been consistent with that idea. It has been exciting because the transformation was from A to Z. We didn't feel we could say we were going to focus on Lovemarks and not lead by example.

TRANSFORMING PAYLESS

Payless is a truly retail account. They really work on promotions. They have 24 promotions a year and do a lot of "Buy One, Get One Half-Price" selling. It's retail at its best.

We work for Payless in nine Latin American countries. Our Lovemarks story is how we were able to persuade the company to develop warmer and closer communications through a campaign that celebrated women, the main shoppers at Payless.

The first thing to do was research, by going to the street and learning from our customers first hand. We worked with close and well-choreographed teamwork. We later introduced Payless to Lovemarks. After outlining the Lovemark qualities and demonstrating the link between emotions and action, we presented shoes to them as an emotional force in women's lives rather than a price-driven category in-store.

FOR PAYLESS

Payless television commercial, Costa Rica.

It's amazing how shoes, an item of such practical purpose, have come to reflect the changes in passions, perspectives, and ideals of our culture. The Greeks wanted to tell us something when they showed Aphrodite, the goddess of love, naked except for a pair of sandals honoring her feet.

INSPIRED BY CONSUMERS

We set out a number of insights we had gathered from consumers.

- The impulse to purchase has nothing to do with the need, it's the emotion of sliding into a new shoe that awakens desire.

- Women buy objects that make them look beautiful and that increase their sensuality, like clothes, beauty products, and shoes.

- The sales sites exert a specific enchantment in the buyer. Saleswomen are like sisters, the salesmen like brothers.

- To buy gives security and satisfaction; it can even produce a brief euphoria.

- It's not what she knows, it's what she feels and desires.

CUALQUIER COLOR ES NUESTRO

SER MUJER ES UN ÉXITO

Marca el paso

NOSOTRAS NOS MAQUILLAMOS

SER MUJER ES UN ÉXITO

Marca el paso

EL TRÁFICO SE DETIENE POR NOSOTRAS

SER MUJER ES UN ÉXITO

Marca el paso

We compared these insights with hard research data. Ninety percent of women buy on impulse. We found that these "expressive" women could become the drivers of more sales if they were convinced to reinforce their loyalty to Payless.

We discovered from our visits to Payless stores that very few women in the stores remembered what they had seen in the window before they had entered. This did not say a great deal for the store displays.

The good news was that most people found the stores comfortable and received good service. This was a shoe store doing everything possible to convert visits into sales. Payless had become a place they liked to visit and find quality and innovation at great prices. We decided that for most Payless customers the store was a "good friend." We wanted to expand this status, with Payless becoming part of the "expressive" woman's life.

PAYLESS AND THE LOVE/RESPECT AXIS

We put Payless and its competitors onto the Love/Respect Axis. Three more important insights resulted.

- Payless had a higher level of Respect among the shoe category players, but on the emotional axis, some of their main competitors enjoyed much better territory.
- While Payless had been in the market only briefly, they had built Respect by communicating their specific product prices, locations, and their self-service format.
- It was clearly time for Payless to work on the emotional link, with elements like Mystery, Sensuality, and Intimacy to achieve higher loyalty and to increase Love for the brand.

CELEBRATING WOMEN

We told Payless we were going to transform them into a feminine "secret weapon." Our objective was to convince shoppers that Payless knows what being a woman means. It was an approach that enhanced the condition of every woman along with many of the advantages they have over men. Our message: "It's a success to be a woman."

This powerful idea moved a retail mind into one that focused on creating relationships and emotional connections. It also meant that Payless focused on women as they've never done before.

Celebrating the customer and her life instead of just presenting her with products and prices appealed to women. Payless, in showing they understood women, created a strong relationship with them. The company talked to women in their language about their interests, rather than in the language and about the interests of business.

The result? By showing an understanding of the cultural differences between the United States and Latin America, Payless was able to connect with Latin American women who enjoyed being motivated by an emotion- rather than a price-based approach. Payless also brought their relationship with their female customers closer to friendship than one just based on transactions. Now the company is seen to be just as concerned about caring, relating, and understanding the needs and intimate feelings of women as it is about selling shoes and accessories. And the result? A double-digit increase in brand awareness.

LEFT: Payless billboards, Costa Rica.

Study screens in your local supermarket. Come up with a way to transform the shopping experience with screens. Patent it!

What frustrates you most when you shop? Work out how a Loremarks store would change those things.

Make a special visit to your favorite store and start a conversation about their Loremarks potential.

Give your imagination a workout. Think about how a music store could use smell to sell CDs or a perfumery could incorporate sound.

Next time you are out of town, visit a bazaar or local market. What could city stores learn from this experience?

FIVE THINGS TO DO TOMORROW

CHAPTER SIX

Form follows feeling

DESIGNING THE WORLD OF LOVEMARKS

In Lovemarks, form follows feeling to create objects imbued with Mystery, Sensuality, and Intimacy. Here's how design can create objects to fall in love with.

Insight interviews
Tom Peters, CEO,
Tom Peters Company

Renzo Rosso, CEO, Diesel

Mary Quant, designer

Arno Penzias, Nobel laureate

Derek Lockwood, Worldwide Director of Design, Saatchi & Saatchi

Love bites
Five things to do tomorrow

feelings, aspirations, and prefer.

Body and Soul

HERMAN MILLER Years ago a friend ran into our office breathlessly, excited about a chair in the furniture shop below. It was, he said, strangely like a hammock. I was soon to run my hands over its sleek, organic curves—I was seeing one of the first Aeron chairs—and within 48 hours I owned one. Nothing has given me such consistent and enduring joy over the years. Its great beauty has never faded. I sit in it secure, knowing that its ergonomic design is protecting me from harm. *Phil, New Zealand*

Lovemarks by design

We are in the era of conspicuous design. Design has never been more accessible. From Stella McCartney's shoes for adidas to the Spinbrush, it's world class design for everyone. A handful of great designers, a band of their followers, and a planet of design-savvy consumers. On the other hand design risks being taken for granted—included in everything and meaning nothing.

I have a briefcase I love so much I have had it repaired time and time again. Is there anything of the original left? Maybe. Is it good design? It is for *me*.

This is why design needs Lovemarks: to connect design skill and talent with human emotion. Design only matters if it brings to light the emotional meaning of a product. Whether designing packaging or wheelchairs, magazines or houses, great designers are inspired by their intimate connections with consumers. Architect Louis Sullivan's famous maxim "form follows function" needs to be rewritten at once. "Form follows feeling" is the inspiration design needs. When we back this inspirational idea with Mystery, Sensuality, and Intimacy we can create design that speaks directly to the heart.

We start this chapter with Tom Peters, a huge advocate of design. Tom is one of the most important business trailblazers of the last 20 years, and joined the Lovemarks adventure at its beginning. As Tom demonstrates, there is a direct connection between Lovemarks and design, and big rewards for companies that put these two powerful forces together. Following Tom is the CEO of a great design inspiration—Diesel. When we talked to Renzo Rosso we discovered a Lovemarks fan from a company that wears love and passion like a second skin.

This chapter also features two outstanding designers from very different fields: Mary Quant and Arno Penzias—a fashion icon and a Nobel laureate. Mary was the first person to inspire me with the power of ideas and design back in 1960s London. Arno, who focused the famous Bell Labs on design for manufacture and customer usability, brings to Lovemarks a sophisticated awareness of engineering, sensuality, and design.

Finally we hear from Derek Lockwood, Worldwide Director of Design for Saatchi & Saatchi. Derek created the emotional impact of our book *Lovemarks* and is also guiding a special designer edition in which each chapter showcases a different designer from our network. KR

On the runway in Milan

Launch of the Lovemarks *book at Giorgio Armani's residence, Milan, Italy.*

coolstuff

I've always appreciated the way Tom Peters has helped spread the Lovemarks message around the world. Tom and I started talking Lovemarks when he sent me a note after buying the book at a store in Edinburgh on a rainy Scottish day. We share a great love of design; here he holds forth on the subject. KR

Lovemarks and design

I would argue, because I'm a design fanatic, that the key to creating a Lovemark is design writ large. Design and Lovemarks, absolutely. To me, for instance, design has as much to do with the process of selling and marketing a car as it does with the actual creation of its shape.

Somebody once asked me, "How did you get into design?" I said, "Well, I don't have an artistic bone in my body," which is really the case. "I got into design not because I thought it was useful from a strategic standpoint to establish a competitive advantage, I got into design because I think cool stuff is cooler than not cool stuff." And that's fundamentally the point.

We use the expression "design-driven" with great regularity, but companies don't have much more of an idea as to what it means than they did five years ago. How do we get beyond the use of the words to a truly design-driven or a design-cultured company? Now that the sexy part of awareness is done, it's 10 years of hard work ahead. It is going to be hard work to establish a design ethos, just like it was hard work 20 years ago to get beyond the idea that quality is cool.

Design and culture

Design has to be a corporate culture. A friend of mine wrote a book about design long before it was a hot topic, and he talked about Olivetti. There design was a cultural given and the CEO was a guy who loved designers. On the one hand design was the cultural ethos of the corporation, while on the other hand they went out of their way to hunt for design stars. Design is both a collective and an individual process.

> " **Now that the sexy part of awareness is done, it's 10 years of hard work ahead.** "
>
> TOM PETERS

Suppose you have a dull and dreary company. Bring in a design superstar and you may get a couple of good products, but you're not going to change the company. If you are serious about design Apple-style, then it has to be a way of life that will necessarily encompass some seriously cool designers. But it's the cultural dimension that's the glue.

It's interesting to contrast Apple with Harley-Davidson. In the case of Harley-Davidson you probably can't name a single designer. Maybe you can, but I sure can't. I've known two of the last three CEOs of Harley-Davidson and they couldn't design their way out of a white paper bag. On the other hand they sure get the phenomenon of creating a company that's driven by design in how it deals with its customers as well as with the product.

Tom Peters—*described by* Business Week *as "Business's best friend and worst nightmare."*

The web as the design of participation

We're beginning to buy an awful lot of things via the web. While the web certainly has a lot of technology behind it that allows us to increasingly do stuff, the web is a pure design medium.

Like many others I've always broken design into two parts: cool per se and usability. Websites that people love have got high doses of both. The web is training people in design. I also think that customers are going to demand a world of "participation," or at least joint ownership, and that plays directly into the hands of design.

Lovemarks in business

IBM is a great example of a Lovemark. Here's a company that has basically changed from being a hardware maker to doing consulting services. IBM's goal, relative to their clients in that world, is to become a Lovemark. What IBM is offering people is an entirely new way of looking at their industry, their company, and how they organize themselves. By my definition that fits an awful lot of the parameters of Lovemarks. Lovemarks apply to professional services as much as to a motorcycle or a Nokia cellphone. It's the same deal.

> ## "The real fun begins when China starts creating Lovemarks ....If you don't understand branding and you have a trillion dollars burning a hole in your pocket, you go out and buy people who do..."
>
> TOM PETERS

If I were sitting down next to Prince Alwaleed, the Citicorp investor, and I were Sam Palmisano from IBM, I'm not sure I'd push the sensuality button. But I sure as hell would be willing to push some of the other buttons, like Mystery, and introduce the idea of Lovemarks.

The business people I meet certainly understand Lovemarks intellectually, so businesses can introduce the notion that we need to appeal to all the senses rather than just take the rational approach. But there is a problem.

There's a line in the *Lovemarks* book about when Kevin first talked about Lovemarks and he watched people try to shrink away and slide down into their chairs at the boardroom table. I was at a meeting recently and talked about Lovemarks along with various other things. Afterwards it was like they bought the act. But while their mouths said they got it, their body language said that they were terrified. It was essentially a repeat of the same phenomenon. You could watch them shifting and stirring and being uncomfortable.

People are grasping for solutions to take them beyond where they've been. Many would buy the fact that branding as we knew it has lost its clout. So they're reaching out. Frankly, the good news is that they are a long way from adopting it. That means the people who do get it have an opportunity to gain some traction relative to their competition. When a lot of people don't get it, that's the best time in the world for the 5 or 10 percent who do.

The whole idea of Lovemarks is getting beyond the brand and understanding that it's not enough. This totally plays into my hands because my message is incredibly simple. You can't compete with Wal-Mart on price, and you can't compete with China on cost. So you'd better do something interesting whether you call it design or whether you call it Lovemarks. I love the Lovemarks term, mostly because it stretches people's minds.

Competing with China

To survive the challenge from China we've got to move up the value-added chain to a degree that couldn't have been imagined even 12 months ago. The real fun begins when China starts creating Lovemarks and gets serious about design. And they are and they will. If you don't understand branding and you have a trillion dollars burning a hole in your pocket, you go out and buy people who do understand. They're not attempting to buy the General Motors of the world, but they are buying second-tier companies. This jacks them into the forefront of these ideas without requiring them to go through all the intermediate steps.

It's already starting to happen. The consumer market in China is growing like crazy. The biggest mall in the United States, which is famous to the point that 747s from Japan fly tourists in, is called the Mall of America. It's outside of Minneapolis and has 2.5 million square feet of sales floor. I read an article that said that the South China Mall, which is somewhere around Dongguan, has 7.1 million square feet of selling space!

China and emotion

The Chinese middle class of 100 or 150 million is probably already near the size of the United States', and certainly a lot bigger than the United Kingdom's. I remember when I first went to China in 1984 the first thing to strike me was that, overnight, they had gone from Mao jackets to over-application of lipstick, the use of reds and greens and bright colors. Having lived with grey for approximately 40 years, they did the inherently human thing and instinctively went for emotional colors.

I don't see the Chinese as being behind the times at all. I assume that, just as in Japan and New Zealand and the United States, young Chinese kids who did not grow up in Mao's China will take to this stuff as instinctively as a kid in Tokyo. There will be as much ear-piercing in Shanghai as there is in San Francisco in short order.

EXPERIENCING THE BRAND

> ## " TO WIN A CONSUMER'S TRUST YOU HAVE TO GET CLOSE TO THEM. "
>
> RENZO ROSSO

Anyone who has looked through Fifty, *the book published for Renzo Rosso's 50th birthday, knows that he shares many of the passions that drive Lovemarks. Diesel has astonished the world many times over with its attitudes, images, and style. Since buying out his partners in the Genius Group, Diesel's owner and founder has made the Diesel brand a part of world youth culture. Diesel's story is a tale of optimism, innovation, and surprise. Here's Renzo responding to our questions on Love and Lovemarks.* KR

AN INSTINCT FOR EMOTION

Diesel has always, and will always, operate independently and instinctively—from the heart more than the head. Diesel is an attitude. It is about being brave, being confident with oneself, wanting to innovate and challenge, and never being satisfied. It means being open to new things and listening to your intuition. That's why emotion is one of our main drivers.

Emotions are also what keep us connected with people—listening and caring for what they think and say, provoking and stimulating them through our communication. We don't sell products, we sell the emotions our products generate. I believe that fashion has to sell a dream. There is also the passion of our people. I'm talking about attention to detail, never being satisfied, always wanting to do more, and the desire to learn and grow which is also based on emotion.

A WORLD OF DIFFERENCE

I like the fact that people are different and love Diesel in many different ways. That's why our store in London is completely different from the one in Paris. But, taking this another step, our store in Covent Garden is also different from the one in King's Road and the one in Carnaby Street. So while these stores have the same spirit they are different. Each one reflects the different tastes of diverse consumers and gives them the possibility of finding the perfect setting for their shopping.

Eclectic personalities with strong, authentic ideas are very Diesel. This is true all over the world—it's an international culture. I like to say that the

Diesel consumer is an intelligent person who does not go for uniforms. They love to select the pieces that are right for them and then mix them with other brands or vintage apparel. Diesel lovers are an amazing global community of many diverse cultures but all sharing a similar outlook.

JUST LIKE A LOVE AFFAIR

To win a consumer's trust you have to get close to them. But you also have to retain a little Mystery to keep them interested. It really is just like a love affair! The way we make our product, the research we do, and the marketing we use is all part of our charm—a sort of holy ceremony. There are no external marketing researchers or cool hunters, we are always the first consumers of what we do. Revealing the secret would mean losing the two pillars of our success—innovation and unpredictability.

Renzo Rosso—*"We don't sell products, we sell the emotions our products generate."*

For me, inviting people to our stores is like inviting friends to my house. I want them to enjoy themselves and to bring their emotions with them. So in our stores people can fully experience the brand with their five senses. They can see and touch the products, enjoy the innovative store design, listen to music and be part of the many activities that take place there—exhibitions, special events, parties. It is about a sense of involvement, entertainment, and fun. That's what makes people want to come back.

Diesel products are a very sensual experience. Touch is essential—how do you feel when you are wearing a product? Does it make you feel sexy? Then there are the textiles and treatments, new fabrics, the smell of the leather, the striking campaign images, and listening to the music that is carefully selected in every store.

Intimacy is reflected in our empathy with our consumers. Diesel communication is appreciated for its originality and unpredictability. We extend this dynamic dialogue when we ask our consumers to become directly involved and express their talents in all our initiatives and events.

> **"MY FIRST INSPIRATION IS ALWAYS IN THE STREET, GOING AROUND LISTENING TO PEOPLE. THIS IS THE MOST IMPORTANT THING I'VE LEARNED."**
>
> RENZO ROSSO

HONESTY AND AUTHENTICITY

I have always believed very strongly in the power of honesty. Our approach is that this is our brand, this is what we think, now you decide if you want to share this kind of life philosophy. We never talk down to people; instead we involve, we challenge, we provoke. Diesel strongly believes in what is genuine and authentic in life.

And that is exactly what we have always communicated. Consider, for example, our claim, "For successful living"—such an exaggerated declaration. But it demonstrates that we do not take ourselves too seriously, that we are able to make fun of conventional advertising.

Our consumers are intelligent and they understand we don't want to impose a way of dressing on them. They know they can add their own creativity to our clothes, by matching them according to their lifestyle and personality. We respect their freedom, and they respect us all the more for it. It's a form of loving—if you love somebody, you put respect first.

THE DIESEL CONSUMER

I don't like the word control and I don't think being controlled by customers means that you are emotionally connected with them. It is like a love affair—the more you take control the less you love the other person, and the less you are loved back. With our consumers I constantly aspire to get their love, and their respect.

As Kevin Roberts says in the first Lovemarks book, "Love cannot be commanded or demanded. It can only be given. Like power, you get love by giving it." Diesel's way of loving customers is through delivering high profile products, innovative communication, and a unique brand experience based on strong emotions. What always drives us is innovation, creativity, unpredictability, and passion.

Our company is now made up of many brand advocates who loved Diesel and then came to work for us. There are also over half a million Diesel fans who have joined the Diesel Cult via our website or by signing up in a Diesel store.

We find that our customers are hungry for information about the brand and we keep them informed through e-newsletters. They can find what is going on across the Diesel planet including our many activities in support of young talents like ITS or Diesel U-Music. We also invite these fans to attend Diesel fashion shows and parties, giving them exclusive gifts and rare collectables, or enhancing their shopping experience by giving them access to products four months ahead of anyone else.

And of course our people keep a high vibe around the brand and this, along with their enthusiasm, feeds our reputation for new and surprising innovation.

FOLLOW THE CONSUMER

I never follow trends. My first inspiration is always in the street, going around listening to people. This is the most important thing I've learned. The ideas and the support of our customers is my first source of inspiration.

Consumers always make the difference—it was consumers buying jeans with holes when stores were reluctant to stock them that created demand for them. If it were not for the consumer's input we would not be here in the way we are today.

Some years ago, we recognized that our consumers were so passionate about the brand that they just wanted more and more. Some people never seem to tire of interacting with the brand. The online Diesel Cult acknowledges the fanatical nature of many of Diesel's brand advocates. These days our consumers are increasingly smart and marketing savvy.

Our presence marketing works on developing activities locally. We organize specific events to gather all our customers in a particular area like in-store events and parties; but also on a global scale, we take advantage of the new possibilities offered by the web. Our consumers can share the feeling of being part of a tribe, while still keeping their unique personalities.

dance all night and work all day

My great friend and first employer Mary Quant was the 1960s for anyone who lived through that exciting decade. Innovative, unconventional, and focused, Mary is a classic Lovemarks story of an art school–trained student who used her passion for individuality and style to create a legend. KR

On creating an icon

When drawing early roughs for the clothes, I'd doodle on the designs as I was working. Once I had the daisy I stuck with it. I used it on mini skirts, belts, tunic dresses, underwear. It just worked terribly well. In the beginning the daisy varied quite a bit. It sometimes had five petals and other times six; sometimes it would be one way up and sometimes another! When we began the cosmetics, the daisy had to be regularized so it could be trademarked. We agreed on five petals with the circle in the center. From then on it was always the same.

Mary Quant *(c.1965)—fashion icon, entrepreneur, and creator of the miniskirt.*

One of the most unusual ways we used it was on one of my favorite dresses, which we called "Banana Split." It had a high neck and a zip that ran right down to below the navel. On one model, Grace Coddington—who is now fashion editor at American *Vogue*—I drew the daisy on her navel so when the zip was pulled down, the daisy would appear. Right from the beginning the daisy was lucky for me. I love that it reads so well from a distance—girls can flash the make-up at each other as a sign of camaraderie. At the same time the daisy implies freshness and vulnerability laced with sexy chic.

Creating Mary Quant as a Lovemark

I so much agree with the idea of Lovemarks. It is all about passion. I started by designing the clothes I wanted myself, for my friends and for art students. I didn't want to grow up because growing up seemed to mean you had to wear very structured clothes and to have a beehive hairdo that was rigid and solid. I wanted clothes I could dance all night and work all day in.

It surprised me when people outside of Chelsea wanted our clothes. When American manufacturers came to our shop Bazaar to buy, saying, "Gee, I am going to manufacture this for America," I felt outraged. Then I quickly realized that we had anticipated a look that was huge and international.

> ## Couturiers at that time used stiff house models and no music. But I was doing a different thing, designing sexy clothes for the way real life is—demo-cratizing fashion.
>
> MARY QUANT

I had wonderful models: Coddington, Jean Shrimpton, Twiggy, Penelope Tree. I was so fortunate to work with such terrific girls. Photographers Bailey, Donovan, Avedon, and others were all my friends. I only used top photographic models to show my collections. Our Knightsbridge shop was designed by Terence Conran. It had an open staircase right down the middle that the models came dancing down, and on which they acted out the clothes—legs, legs, legs prancing down the stairway with jazz and rock music, photographers flashing from below. Couturiers at that time used stiff house models and no music. But I was doing a different thing, designing sexy clothes for the way real life is—democratizing fashion.

The Mary Quant look

I wanted to design a complete look from head to toe. We had the miniskirt and mini-skirted dresses, so I needed tights in colors to match the skinny rib sweaters that went with them. Pantyhose did not exist then—stocking manufacturers didn't have the machines—so I persuaded theatrical manufacturers to make them in the sweater colors: Colman's mustard yellow, plum, ginger, and black. I met Vidal Sassoon, who was cutting hair in a completely new way with architectural, asymmetric shapes. He cut my hair in his famous five-point cut, and most of the models' as well. Everything looked right except the makeup.

Mary Quant makeup

Cosmetics had become stuck. Cosmetic companies were huge and international and saw no reason to change with fashion. They saw lipstick as only ever being red, pink, or orange, and nail polish the same. The look was hard and lacquered and sold by dragon-like ladies.

As an art student I was using my Caran d'Ache crayons and watercolor paint box and brushes to do my makeup. I was merging the colors. You could achieve a natural look so that no one realised you were wearing makeup at all.

Then I saw Shrimpton and Coddington using foot-long brushes from stage makeup suppliers. This moved my thinking again. I wanted to develop a makeup collection that used different colors, different textures, different ways of application, and all in boxes you could carry around in your handbag.

I talked with cosmetic manufacturers who got excited, but they were only interested in doing a one-season promotion. Then a marvellous American cosmetic manufacturer, Stanley Picker, came into our garage studio and told me he would show me how to do it technically. We got so excited we started work that night. I wanted the packaging to be black, white, and silver and the product to be color. We spent nearly two years developing the Mary Quant cosmetic brand. It was a completely new approach to makeup. When we launched in 1966 it was the most frighteningly stunning success.

Getting in at the deep end

I remember trying to persuade the laboratory and the chemists to develop a waterproof mascara. I loved to swim and I loved to go the movies—but if they were weepies you got your mascara smudged all round your face!

I talked to the manufacturers about why making waterproof mascara was important and they just didn't see the need. They said, "Why do you want it? Women swim with their heads out of the water." I of course said, "That's because of their makeup!" I got them to start work and they did it—they developed a waterproof mascara.

When we were testing it I was on holiday in the South of France. I was so surprised to find these chic French women following me into the changing rooms and asking, "What is that mascara you are wearing? It stays on." Then I realized we had a real success.

Our first waterproof mascara was so waterproof it was hard to take off. Girls used to boast about how many days they could keep it on! We had to modify it and we developed a special remover we called Lift Off.

My husband Alexander Plunket Greene was a brilliant and natural marketing man who started the famous names that were always dashing or amusing. One of the first was for our foundation, Starkers, and it progressed from there. Cry Baby waterproof mascara, bras were Booby Traps, and tights were Bacon Savers. Why? Because they saved your bacon!

Engineered

Arno Penzias' life has been a string of remarkable achievements. He was awarded the 1978 Nobel prize in physics for discovering the faint background radiation remaining from the "big bang" explosion that gave birth to the universe. Arno was Vice President and Chief Scientist of Bell Labs and is the author of many books, including Harmony in which he advocates for consumers being partners in the design process. This extended version of his contribution to Lovemarks gives an even deeper insight into the emotional savvy of this great physicist. KR

> " Somebody once said, describing a woman, that her face was perfect except for one little flaw, and it was that flaw that made her beautiful. "
>
> ARNO PENZIAS

Lovemarks and perfection

Lovemarks is an extension of brands by taking them to a higher level. It's a marketing concept, a way to help people in the business of creating value for potential customers, present or future. It's a more powerful framework in which to define commercial value. But this doesn't mean everything in the world has to fit into a Lovemark frame. You can love lots of things which aren't Lovemarks. I love my wife, but she's not a brand extension. The same with my overcoat, or a tree I sit under. These aren't Lovemarks even though I love them. They aren't part of the branding, marketing, and product definition process. It is important for us to understand the necessity for focusing in some cases and restricting the range of choices. Otherwise you really can't collect meaningful data.

Somebody once said, describing a woman, that her face was perfect except for one little flaw, and it was that flaw that made her beautiful. There has to be this little kind of twist or eccentricity. Perfect things can't be Lovemarks. A Lovemark has to be something that's a little off-beat in some wonderful way.

Consumers owning Lovemarks

I'm not sure that the consumers ultimately decide. The new Volkswagen Beetle and the Mini were trying to be Lovemarks, and they made it. But they were aimed at a Lovemark kind of market. You have to love this thing because it's kind of small and cheeky. People were in love with Oldsmobiles for years, but not like they are with Harley-Davidsons. Once Oldsmobile

for love

started having problems, people went elsewhere. I have this mental picture that the ultimate Lovemark is a special possession. You don't just possess it in the commonplace sense of that word, but possessing that special thing becomes part of how you define yourself.

Lovemarks and excess

Do I have Lovemarks? Of course. I have one watch I really like, and some people, men especially, have 50 watches they don't like. I have shirts that I love so much my wife forces me to throw them out. Wonderful things are not necessarily excessive. On the other hand I think a lot of branding is. Somebody gold-plating a Rolls Royce or putting a swimming pool into a 50-foot stretch limo, that's not a Lovemark. That's not what Lovemarks are about. I don't think Lovemarks have to do with excess. They could, but I suspect that when something goes in that direction it stops being a Lovemark anyway.

Engineering and Lovemarks

Great engineering can get you near to being a Lovemark, and sometimes great engineering even gets you into the Lovemark box. Certainly the most beautifully engineered things in the world move into that category. High-end Italian cars become such a sensual experience that people fall in love with them. You can get there by design and engineering together.

The early Vespas were built by aeroplane folks who were good at bending metal. The difference between an aeroplane and cars in the early days was that with cars the skin was put on a frame, whereas with an aeroplane you don't want the weight, so the body of the aeroplane has always been a strength. The Vespa was designed with a shield in the front and one behind the wheel to protect the feet, so people could ride it without straddling it. Because it satisfied a need it became a classic product that people loved. To me it is a great example of how a Lovemark came from engineering.

Arno Penzias—*thought leader, scientist, and innovator.*

BEYOND

As Worldwide Director of Design for Saatchi & Saatchi Derek Lockwood has the job of bringing Lovemarks into every aspect of our design work. Great design can turn desire into delight, an essential step in the Lovemarks journey. KR

DESCRIPTION

TOWARDS GOOD DESIGN

I've always believed that good designers are the people who played around with stuff as kids. They were always pulling things apart, figuring out how they work, then putting them back together. When they got older they began to apply their own individual perceptions, experiences, and understanding—their own ideas and flair are added to that accumulated practical knowledge.

Design is a language and is the physical manifestation of ideas. Design, and the implementation of design, delivers multi-sensory stimulation that gives tangibility to concepts. It is a process that brings ideas to life.

Whether we are talking concept visualization, a sketch, or the structural engineering behind a new product, design allows communication to take place on many levels. If, when talking to somebody, you draw a picture of what you are describing, even if it's just a box with an arrow and a squiggle, their ability to understand what is being discussed takes on a whole new dimension. In this way communication through design is self-evident.

This language of design grabs the senses. Beautifully-designed products demand to be touched—the form of a bottle, the rich and intriguing imagery of a pack, the view into a store through the window, the drape of clothes on a rack. At its best, design is irresistible.

Derek Lockwood—*passionate believer in the power of design to make emotional connections with consumers.*

> ## " AS AN IDEAS COMPANY, DESIGN IS A CRUCIAL MEANS FOR US TO ENGAGE CLIENTS, CONSUMERS, SUPPLIERS, AND PRODUCERS WITH OUR IDEAS. "
>
> DEREK LOCKWOOD

But the language of design is not just about the senses. It is also about stories, insight, and discovery. It translates ideas from conception to production, through to use and advocacy. Include an intriguing backstory or tiny details that reveal themselves over time, and design takes on an even more powerful purpose: the ability to reward consumers time and time again. How often have you heard the excitement in someone's voice as they discover something new about a product they have owned for some time?

YIN AND YANG

Recently I have been working in China and have been amazed at the Chinese ability to create prototypes and solve complex design production problems. It's clear to me that the more it is commissioned to make things for the rest of the world, the more China will build expertise and knowledge. And, of course, the more curiosity and the desire to experiment will flourish.

Visiting Beijing, it is easy to see how traditional Chinese design is quickly being assimilated by young Chinese designers. The lessons of a great traditional design practice are finding a new purpose as a foundation for contemporary products and brands. To back up this revitalization, in Beijing, a new Technology and Design course has been introduced into the national curriculum. It's not hard to see that all this activity and creative curiosity is going to place China as a design leader early in this century.

For example, contemporary Chinese art has made an impressive impact on the global art scene over the last three or four years. People like performance artists Cai Guo-Qiang and Zhang Huan are pushing the conceptual boundaries with fantastic works of imagination, endurance, and even pyrotechnics.

The future of design in China needs to be considered in terms of the traditional principles of Yin and Yang. Think of Yang as China's massive production capability and Yin as the growing desire for self-expression, blossoming from greater connectivity and spontaneity. I believe it is this potent combination that will shape the Chinese contribution to worldwide design.

DESIGN AND SAATCHI & SAATCHI

As an Ideas Company, design is a crucial means for us to engage clients, consumers, suppliers, and producers with our ideas. That's why design permeates our business. Ideas are at the heart of everything we do, so we regard design as a capability. Design becomes a practical discipline working alongside other creative inputs.

Like everything in our business, design is measured by its tangible outcomes, and the way we conceptualize those outcomes is always based on connectivity—between creatives and business managers, between the ideas and the client, between the researcher and the consumers, the designer and the engineer. Design becomes a means to express and translate ideas into a language that can be shared. Only then can we engage consumers with the kind of understanding and insights that will help generate long-term loyalty.

The domain of design we are working in is specifically structured around how to motivate and inspire consumers throughout the purchasing process. We call it Shopper-Led Design. Our goal is to deliver results that transform business through our specializations in identity, business design, packaging, and product innovation. In other words, design that performs at every consumer touchpoint.

Shopper-Led Design starts with the understanding that the consumer's freedom to choose sits at the center of everything we do. A purchase is an opportunity that begins with unfulfilled needs and desires. From this foundation we take a journey that includes driving awareness, stimulating attraction, promoting action, inspiring advocacy, and leading consumers to Love.

"Lovemarks" in Chinese calligraphy

Look at the coolest designs around and head in the opposite direction. You'll meet everyone else on the way back.

Evaluate your cards, labels, signage, website. Do they sing Lovemarks? If not, start playing a new tune.

What's your favorite design object? Has it been nominated on Lovemarks.com? If so, add to the love. If not, do it now.

Great designers tap into myths, metaphors, and stories. Think about what a mythical store display might look like.

Choose five magazines at your local store and work out the elements that made the design "speak" to you.

CHAPTER SEVEN

Love one day at a time

LOVEMARKS AND SUSTAINABILITY

The role of business is to make the world a better place. This chapter foregrounds sustainability as the bottom line and introduces Lovemarks as a way to realize that dream.

Insight interviews

Mary Robinson, former President of Ireland and United Nations High Commissioner for Human Rights

Inoue Masao, Chief Engineer of the Prius, Toyota Motor Company

Mike Pratt, Dean, Waikato Management School

Roger Downer, University of Limerick

John Wareham, business mentor and author

Mika, dancer and performer

Love bites

Aqua, Indonesia
Students in Free Enterprise
Amul, India
Five things to do tomorrow

NEWMAN'S OWN This company totally inspires me—I've never known a company to give away ALL of its profits to charity and education in the way that Newman's Own does. Their Newman-O's cookies and sauces symbolize homegrown quality for me—like having the deliciousness of Paul Newman's legendary film work all tucked into something you can eat! How can I resist, when I know that every delicious bit of cookie is being offered back to charity? An inspiring $150 million-plus in funds given away to help others is what the American dream is all about. Their marketing humor only adds to their appeal—It started as a joke and got out of control—who can beat that? Yes, charity gone wild! I just love this company's attitude and service to the world. A down-home model for corporate America. *Ragani, United States*

The forever revolution

The great challenge before us is to build sustainable enterprises. In a world that has finite resources it is critical that every business looks to its processes and products as being sustainable in the long term. This is as important for small corner stores as it is for huge steel companies. Command and control won't work in a world of global proximity, transparency, and accountability. We must act now to unleash and inspire the potential around us.

Progress has always been led by enterprising individuals and fortunately I see more people taking up the challenge and opportunity. Not just rock stars, retired heads of state, business leaders, and sports legends, but also everyday heroes who get up off the couch, spark an idea, and start something new.

The best way for business to make the world a better place is the power of one. The determination of one person as a leader or as part of a group—the power of each individual to make change happen. The very different stories of Aqua water, the Toyota Prius, Turn Your Life Around (TYLA), Amul dairy cooperative, and Students in Free Enterprise (SIFE) show how this journey can be taken. These people create opportunities, environments, experiences, and cultures that build and transform lives. They drive for the tipping points between the possible and the real. And they do what's right.

The role of business is to make the world a better place. What a challenge! The connection with Lovemarks is fast and direct. A precondition for Lovemark status is products that are designed, manufactured, and sold from an ethical, sustainable, and healthy context. Lovemarks must have Respect as well as Love.

This chapter features five remarkable people who share the conviction that we can act to make the world a better place. Mary Robinson brings new ideas and hope to those who are left out of our newly-connected world. In Japan, Inoue Masao is making a real contribution to the sustainability of the planet through the development of hybrid technology. My close colleagues, partners, and friends, Professors Mike Pratt and Roger Downer, contribute their thoughts on how sustainability can transform business. And the inimitable John Wareham shares his perspective on life, business, and making a difference. KR

Launch of the Lovemarks *book, Moscow, Russia.*

Champion of

> ❝ **Never doubt that a small group of thoughtful, committed citizens can change the world. Indeed, it's the only thing that ever has.** ❞
>
> MARGARET MEAD

I first met Mary Robinson in New York and immediately connected with her principled and pragmatic passion for human rights as a key role in a sustainable future for our world. Saatchi & Saatchi were able to support Mary's tireless work with Realizing Rights: The Ethical Globalization Initiative (EGI) which she set up after leaving the United Nations as High Commissioner for Human Rights. Realizing Rights is committed to the idea that a world connected by trade and technology must also be bound by common values based on a shared understanding of human rights. This is how to help develop equitable and effective responses to real-world problems. We have kept in touch through our joint love of Ireland and my connections with Limerick University. Mary, who was nominated one of TIME magazine's 100 Most Influential People of 2005, is a perpetual optimist who is taking on some of the most difficult challenges the world faces. Find out more about Realizing Rights at realizingrights.org. KR

Together we stand

A great example of women joining together to exercise leadership for a better future is the African Women's Millennium Initiative (AWOMI). The initiative draws together many grassroots women's organizations mostly involved in local enterprises and cooperatives. They produce crafts, textiles, and artifacts, and try to find markets for them, and they are involved in local community development.

You've got women who are not only working in their own small economic sector and helping themselves, their families, and their communities, but who are also networking together to have a stronger voice.

Ten years ago those women would not have wanted to make an impact at the international level. Their voice is now heard at the General Assembly of the United Nations in New York. Now they are thinking and working locally, while knowing that they must also interact globally.

Another example of a women's self-development organization is SEWA (Self-Employed Women's Association) in India. They are recognizing the power of many. They have done incredible work in providing services for poor women like savings and credit, health care, and child care. By setting up their own bank, which they own collectively, these women can access the resources

humanity

they need to be successfully self-employed and support their families. The result is that millions of women have generated cash flow into their homes.

Language and metaphor

To make emotional connections you need a language that touches people. I found this to be so important when I was President of Ireland. When I wanted to connect with the wider Irish family outside of Ireland, I put a light at the window of my official residence. It was a symbol that we cared and that we wanted to make a connection. It was hugely powerful in generating emotion.

People from all over the world visited the residence and told me that they would "love to see the light." I'd point it out, and often when I turned back, I would find the person had tears coming down their cheeks. It really did strike a very deep chord.

When I was trying to help the peace process in Northern Ireland, language and metaphor were central. I often spoke about extending the hand of friendship to both communities, and I would share stories of what a former paramilitary local Protestant had said to me, and what a woman in the Falls Road had said to me. It's partly telling stories, but it's also touching people with reality.

I'm doing the same thing in Mali and Mozambique. Talking about the impact of trade on the lives of individual people is a powerful way to get the message across. I've found that when you bring in the human dimension people do understand. It's the power of the story—you've got to touch people's hearts.

The role of business

Business can be a force either for good or for ill; it has been both. Modern governments have less power today because they have privatized a significant range of the services they used to provide in health, education, and even justice. Governments still have primary responsibility, but power has shifted toward the corporate sector. Business now needs to be more actively engaged in human rights, and this is beginning to happen. There have been a number of success stories and I have been encouraged at the changes in attitudes from many business leaders who, in their turn, have been surprised and encouraged at both the process and the results.

Mary Robinson—*humanitarian and unswerving advocate for the disenfranchised of the world.*

AQUA IN ACEH

Lovemark companies are always alert to opportunities where they can help make a difference. Our client in Indonesia, Aqua, showed this spirit following the tragic 2004 Boxing Day Tsunami. Here's the story told by Anthony Plant, CEO of the Hong Kong office of Saatchi & Saatchi. KR

On December 26, 2004, Indonesia suffered a greater loss of life and devastation from the Asian tsunami than any other nation in the region.

People around the world struggled to come to terms with the scale of the disaster and to understand what would be the most useful help and assistance to provide to the nations affected. Aqua quickly realized that the resources at its disposal were essential to getting what people needed more urgently than anything else—drinking water.

Galvanizing the company into action by appealing to the compassion and goodwill of all of its employees, Aqua distributed over one million bottles of drinking water to the worst-hit areas of Aceh province in Indonesia.

Aqua recognizes its place in the hearts of Indonesian consumers and the responsibility that comes with that, while across the world Aqua became associated with the worldwide efforts to sustain life in one of the worst natural disasters in modern history.

13 January 2005—Aqua water being delivered to Suexeeka, Aceh province, Indonesia following the Asia Tsunami on Boxing Day 2004.

BEING THERE

Our client Toyota is leading the way in producing vehicles that will help make the world cleaner and more fuel efficient. Their flagship hybrid car, the Prius, has received accolades from around the world and its drivers are fierce protectors of its Lovemark status. Inoue-san probably knows the Prius better than anyone. KR

Creating the car for the future

Toyoda Eiji and Toyoda Kiichiro, the leaders of the Toyoda family and founders of the company, always wanted to produce special cars. They were always trying to find the best way to make a contribution to society.

Toyota produces 6 million cars annually, and in the world 60 million cars are produced each year. The number of cars actually on the road is almost ten times this figure, so about 500 million cars altogether. Imagine what quantity of emissions those cars are producing! Surely it's not going to be good for us for those cars to keep on producing exhaust fumes.

In the latter half of the 1980s and beginning of the 1990s, the founders of the Toyota company and all the engineers realized there needed to be a fundamental, drastic answer to the environmental issue. The challenge was to decide what would be the most suitable type of car to build for the next generation. They concluded that they should be making a car that would create as light a burden on the environment as possible. They thought that would be a sustainable way of manufacturing.

Small, incremental developments in technology wouldn't provide the answer. There would need to be some drastic changes. There were a number of possible solutions, and we followed a range of different pathways. One of them was the hybrid engine, which we thought had excellent prospects.

In 1997 the first Prius was launched. The Toyota management team took a risk with the early release of this hybrid technology. But by doing this we set ourselves apart from competitors. At the same time, customers trusted us because of our history of making things right. They also developed an affectionate attitude towards the company for trying something difficult and complicated, which no other carmakers were trying.

Building a Lovemark: the Prius

This is a complex thing to explain, but the uniqueness of the Prius is a feeling beyond measurement.

Figures are important, but we also value how you, the driver, and your body feel, too. We talk about quietness. Noise can be measured by figures, but there's also the quietness that you feel within your body.

There are things that you cannot get from data but that you find out when you actually drive the car. The human ear—and the body—are the best sensors of all. There is nothing, no machine, which can replace them.

When we're talking about "quietness," there are many, many sounds to listen for—the sound of the engine, the motor, the tires on the road. When you drive the car, you get the sound from the wind passing by. But what about the air-conditioning inside of the car? These are tiny things. You can't really measure it with figures. But these small sounds can really irritate a driver.

When you drive a car you need to feel safe. Like in a hotel, where you feel quite safe and comfortable, but at the same time you should be able to feel totally relaxed, just as when you're driving in an open space. The feeling we're trying to go for is a real sense of ease when you're actually driving.

Inoue Masao—*putting Toyota on the cutting edge of hybrid engine technology.*

> ## 66 I learned a great deal from my mother. To gain the trust of your customer, you have to trust your customer first. 99
>
> INOUE MASAO

Before joining the development team, I purchased a Prius, and then a year ago I got a new one. I too feel that I'm doing some good for the environment.

Innovative engineering

For my own professional satisfaction I want to surprise customers. The second thing, more importantly, is how can I be useful to society?

As an engineer, I have the responsibility and authority for the development of a particular car. I want to do something nobody has done before, and to be first to create something and not just mimic others.

I would also like to produce a car, a very popular car, that everyone wants to buy. At the end of the day, the car has to be bought by customers. It doesn't matter how good the quality is, if it's not appealing to people or is too expensive, people won't buy it. We have to develop a car that people will actually buy. And I think a car's desirability lies in the fact that you can drive it exactly the way you want.

We may offer a very good and very environmentally friendly car, but if no one buys it, it goes nowhere. So we have to base our ideas and philosophies about what we should make around our knowledge of what will make it attractive to our customers.

My passion for cars...

When I was 10 years old I drove a car for the first time. I wasn't allowed to do so, but I drove my mother's car. I thought that was great fun.

Of course I couldn't actually drive an ordinary car on the road—so I wanted to make a car I could drive. When I was in the fifth grade I made an electric car. This shows you how much I liked cars! And the second car I built was just too fast, and I couldn't drive it myself—so my school teacher drove it.

Each year for four years, I entered the Suzuka racing circuit competition run by *Car Graphic* magazine. Every second Sunday I would be stuck in my own garage, building cars. My fingernails were completely black and oily. During the week, when I was working in the office, I tried to clean up my dirty fingernails. Then in the weekend I would mess them up again.

...and customers

Toyoda Kiichiro engendered mutual admiration, respect, and the love that is based on mutual trust. Lots of people in the world are doing this.

My family ran a business, a pet shop selling birds—pigeons and budgies. Mainly my mother ran the place. There were some very nice customers, but also some awful ones, and I once said to my mother, "Ugh, I don't want to serve that customer."

My mother persuaded me that you shouldn't say something like that. She said, "Customers, if you doubt them, they will never trust you! You really need to trust customers and then try your hardest to serve them."

I learned a great deal from my mother. To gain the trust of your customer, you have to trust your customer first.

TRANSFORMING
BUSINESS

The drive towards sustainable enterprise is a passion I share with Mike Pratt and Roger Downer. I think of the "enterprise" in the term "sustainable enterprise" as akin to enterprising—innovative, clever, flexible. We won't solve our problems with old-style thinking. That's what caused the problems in the first place. We need to find a fresh understanding of sustainable business success in a connected world. This understanding needs to be inspired by long-term economic, social, environmental, and cultural success. Innovative countries like Ireland and New Zealand can lead the way. Mike is at the University of Waikato in New Zealand, and Roger was President of the University of Limerick in Ireland from 1998 to 2006. They are ideally located to pursue edge ideas and action. KR

PROFITS, PEOPLE, AND THE PLANET

MIKE: The traditional notions of market economies are being transformed through sustainability thinking. It amounts to nothing less than a fundamental change in the way the world does business. It's even more profound than the quality movement of the 1980s. That was all about efficiency and effectiveness whereas the new wave of sustainability is much more about doing what's right in the first place.

Senior business leaders are recognizing that the singular pursuit of profit is counterproductive. If you create profit but don't respect people, there's no one left to buy your product—except in the very short term. If you don't respect the planet, then you don't even have a context in which to operate your company. Certainly business should be concerned about profit, people, and the planet, but in a way that doesn't necessarily privilege any single one of them. They're all interdependent and each can be enhanced through business.

I think that increasingly, organizations whose main purpose is to make as much money as possible are not likely to do very well. People are not going to want to work for an organization if they don't connect with its purpose. Businesses need to have an inspiring purpose to which people can feel emotionally committed. This is why sustainability matters, because people are inspired when sustainability principles are embedded into the purpose of the organization. For example, if your purpose is to create wealth and well-being for people, organizations, and society, then that will be positively embraced within the organization's development.

SUSTAINABLE ENTERPRISE

ROGER: One of the great oxymorons that has come into popular use is "sustainable development." I consider it oxymoronic because most people associate development with growth and of course it is just not possible to have continuous growth in the long-term, sustainable or not. Trees don't keep growing to heaven; in time they reach a steady state. What we should be talking about is "development for sustainability."

Sustainable enterprises demand much more responsible corporate practice and governance. Ultimately I think it is the shareholders who are going to dictate the type of company they wish to own, and this should lead to a much more responsible form of business.

The challenges of achieving sustainable enterprises certainly cannot be underestimated, but shareholders are starting to take a much greater interest in what's happening. Triple bottom-line reporting, with social and environmental contributions being described along with financial performance, is becoming increasingly well-developed. This is going to become a major marketing advantage to companies who will be proud to advertise this kind of activity.

I am very interested in the idea of an "ecological footprint." This is the amount of land required to support the lifestyle enjoyed by people in a particular country. When we look at these footprints globally, we find that the Western lifestyle can only continue if much of the third world remains impoverished. This is the cost of growth in developed countries. It is also why such growth is not sustainable.

Mike Pratt (top) and *Roger Downer* (bottom)—*committed to making the world a better place.*

> ## 66 TO ME THE KEY FACTORS ARE LOYALTY AND VALUES. WHAT WE'RE TALKING ABOUT HERE IS HAVING THE MORAL COURAGE TO DO WHAT YOU KNOW IS RIGHT, AND THE COURAGE TO NOT DO WHAT YOU KNOW IS WRONG. 99
>
> ROGER DOWNER

The world is not sustainable if there are 2 billion people living on about two dollars per day. Talking about it is not enough. We need a carefully integrated strategy that starts with the recognition of the problem. If there are any trends that encourage me, I think the most important is the recognition that is now being given to global poverty. Now we have to start developing a unified approach and looking at ways in which we can encourage investment in the Third World. Currently there are serious constraints around starting enterprises there. These constraints include corrupt governments, poor infrastructure, and poor education. Any aid or debt relief should be directed at overcoming these barriers to enterprise development. An important caveat is that companies setting up in these countries must pay competitive wages and not see them as a source of cheap labor.

EMBRACING SUSTAINABILITY

ROGER: To me the key factors are loyalty and values. What we're talking about here is having the moral courage to do what you know is right, and the courage to not do what you know is wrong. If you do this out of a burning desire to make your business succeed in a responsible manner which considers societal needs, then perhaps that is Love. But really we're talking about a value system that embraces sustainability as a means of creating a better world for all people.

MIKE: Lovemarks need both Love and Respect so that businesses can bring emotion and function together at the point of purchase. It helps people understand the process of consumer choice and, at a larger level, how to organize corporations and develop marketing programs. The risk is in the bottom right-hand quadrant of the Love/Respect Axis. You slap emotion over a product, brand, or an organization that isn't respected in so far as its purpose is concerned, and it becomes massively counter-productive. You have to be big on both Love and Respect.

THE CHALLENGE TO GLOBAL BRANDS

MIKE: The bigger the global brand and the more of an impact it has, the more likely it is to come under attack on its sustainability record. There are many organizations acting badly in either social or environmental areas but they are rarely put in the spotlight. The ones who are vulnerable are the apparent leaders. Their performance is no better or worse than many others, but by targeting the big brands the critics get the biggest impact. And although the biggest global brands are the most exposed, they also have the most potential for doing good by doing right.

Consumers really do care about this. When you examine the factors that make up consumers' brand choices, it turns out that there are real benefits for companies following sustainability principles. Research by Holt, Quelch, and Taylor on how global brands compete, published in the *Harvard Business Review* in September 2004, makes this very clear. After surveying consumers in 12 countries, the researchers identified three stand-out reasons why people choose global brands. These three factors explain roughly 64 percent of the variation in brand preferences worldwide.

The first was the signals they picked up on about the brand's quality, which are clearly associated with Respect factors like innovation and technology. The second reason was more emotional and related-to elements like stories and where the brand came from. These are clearly connected with the Lovemark qualities of Mystery and Intimacy. The third reason consumers gave for choosing a brand, accounting for 8 percent of global brand preference, was how they perceived the organization's level of corporate social responsibility—or what I would call sustainable enterprise. This might not sound like a lot, but 8 percent is hugely significant when you are dealing with products that are essentially indistinguishable.

Sustainability is not just about environmental, social, and economic issues—it also has a cultural dimension. In the face of globalization, societies seek to preserve their cultural values and community identity, and still participate in the global economy. The global economy is strengthened by cultural identity. In a global context, where it is increasingly hard to differentiate products, the cultural identity of those products becomes an important part of their value proposition.

Radical

Through Students in Free Enterprise (SIFE), university students worldwide bring to life educational, ethical, and business-savvy programs that improve the standard of living and quality of life for others. These students develop solutions to real-world challenges in their own communities and, in the process, they are irrevocably changed. In helping others they realize their own potential to make a difference. I have been able to play a small part in this great success story. Through my association with the University of Waikato, New Zealand, I have been involved in the sponsorship of the Waikato SIFE team that has won the New Zealand national competition and then the SIFE World Cup.

It takes many of us a lifetime to learn how to do business in a real and meaningful way that touches hearts and minds. These radical optimists seem to do it intuitively, and are ready to step up as tomorrow's business leaders. Jens Mueller, Regional Vice President and Manag-ing Director of SIFE Asia, gives the background to the SIFE story. KR

The SIFE team from Waikato Management School, Waikato University, after winning the 2003 SIFE World Cup.

Optimists

SIFE's global growth has been exponential. Since its beginnings as a small non-profit organization in the United States in 1975, SIFE has flourished. It now operates in over 40 countries, comprises a worldwide team of thousands of students, and has gained support from hundreds of global and local businesses. More than 1,400 university campuses across almost every continent have established a SIFE team.

Each year, SIFE teams are challenged to develop community outreach projects that can shift paradigms. Students create programs with a focus on educating others about market economics, entrepreneurship, personal financial success skills, and business ethics.

The teams then compete for the title of most effective program nationally and the best go on to the SIFE World Cup. It's a challenge that can produce astounding results.

In 2004, Shanghai International Services University developed a program called Rainbows in the Field, in the rural villages of Yancheng, Yixing, and Chengde. The project assisted farmers in creating sustainable businesses by providing direct access to education and basic resources, such as seeds and supplies. They learned new techniques and a new way of looking at the world. One Chinese farmer remarked that Rainbows in the Field had helped him to "earn a brighter future."

Other inspiring SIFE projects include savings schemes in Ghana, Internet games to learn the value of free economies in Poland, and videos on improving business ethics in the United Kingdom.

"We feel like we're changing the world by changing our own communities," said one student at the 2005 SIFE World Cup.

The transformative qualities of SIFE work magic in the world. SIFE empowers young people to become leaders and to focus their energies on creating better communities with a sustainable, long-term focus. Their efforts have a profound effect on at-risk youth, students of all ages, and small and large businesses, turning SIFE students into heroes in their own communities.

Bashir Hassan, the faculty advisor at United States International University in Kenya, has also seen the long-term benefits for his SIFE students.

"Within two weeks of graduation, all of my SIFE students last year were hired by Kenyan companies. In a country that has more than 60 percent unemployment, that was a miracle," he says.

The signature of SIFE is its commitment to the importance of relationships—with peers, communities, and global businesses alike.

There can be no sustainable effort without a close, lasting relationship that goes beyond the ups and downs of individual products and services. SIFE teaches that a deep and meaningful understanding of community needs is essential to present innovative ideas.

This understanding is taken into the business world when the students graduate, helping to make a real difference to the global community.

The ability to make emotional connections with people sets companies apart. If they can reach into other people's lives and hearts, then that is worth something.

Transformational

> ## Love and business can and do mix. That is the direction in which we are traveling now, and very quickly too. I think Love is the way to go.

JOHN WAREHAM

My friend John Wareham is a study in paradox. A shrewd business leader yet a sensitive novelist and poet, a devastated stutterer who became an award-winning orator and lecturer, and a connoisseur of high-riding executives and the lowliest of prison inmates alike. How did this self-confessed wiry little white guy ever wind up teaching predominantly black audiences How to Break Out of Prison—*the title of one of his most fascinating books—in such places as Rikers Island, the world's largest penal colony? Every week John puts his time and energy into programs at New York's toughest prisons, giving hope to people who might otherwise be lost. John has an instinct for the power of language and how it can create transformational and sustainable ideas. John was born in New Zealand, lives in New York, and works around the world.* KR

The power of language and ideas

Working with inmates at a prison like Rikers, you can either sit opposite someone and say, "Look, here's the problem. You got harmed as you were growing up and, because of that, you think the wrong things and you do the wrong things." You can say that, or you can say, "I'd like you to look at this poem," and let them come to these ideas by themselves.

A friend told me a wonderful poem that I use. The last lines are, "You will not understand, but will endure; snakebit, and never dreaming of a cure." I go through the poem with them and they can't make any sense of it at all. But as soon as I say, "Well, who's been bitten here?" and we go around the room and speak about the snake, it turns out that everybody's been bitten.

I introduce ideas that these men have never had before, and in a form that they at first don't quite understand. Then I help them to the truth that is within.

These are ideas that go home. It would be completely ineffective if I stood up and said, "You guys shouldn't commit crimes any more." That just wouldn't work. The hardest thing is to get people to see how they can exist out of jail. But you can't exist out of jail if you don't know how you got in.

ideas

Readings at Rikers

I use Shakespeare, Freud, Oscar Wilde, and other great writers in my classes at Rikers because that's where the great language is and the great ideas are. I carefully select the biggest ideas that I can find, the most transformational ideas, and share them. They may come from Plato, they may come from Freud, they may come from a contemporary person, or whoever, but ultimately they all lead toward the same result: to help people see where they fit in the world. I've found that this approach works with inmates, with executives, with just about everyone.

Great ideas have a life of their own, and every individual with something worthwhile to say or do can make a giant difference. I'm a fan of the Niels Bohr line, "The fluttering of a butterfly's wings in Hong Kong can affect the roll of a billiard ball in New York." We can all be that butterfly. If we cannot be true to ourselves within a particular organization, we should either change it or leave it.

John Wareham—*perceived how much prison inmates and executives have in common.*

Love and business

Sustainability sprang from the work of the quality pioneer W. Edwards Deming. He was the first to realize that the missing component in industry was an authentic commitment to humanity—both workers and consumers—and that a quality product was an instrument for building trust and Love.

Business must address the real needs of the consumer by creating high-quality products. When they seek quality before profit, and when they seek sustainable profits, true prosperity will follow. Love and business can and do mix. That is the direction in which we are traveling now, and very quickly too. I think Love is the way to go.

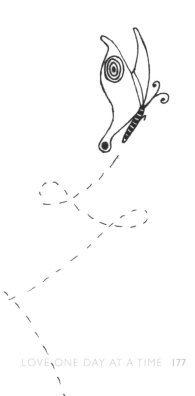

Turn Your Life

> ## " When the mind is optimistic it tends to accept challenges, to move, develop, and change. "
>
> MIKA

A fundamental belief of my life is that everyone has potential. My work with TYLA (the Turn Your Life Around Trust) springs from that conviction. We find again and again that attention, commitment, and love can expand lives that have become narrow and without vision. In my experience this is the only way to transform young people who come from very difficult personal and family situations.

TYLA was started in Auckland, New Zealand 10 years ago, and operates a youth development program in partnership with the New Zealand Police. It is designed to prevent at-risk youth from drifting into a life of crime. I've watched kids from the most difficult situations arrive at TYLA camps and be transformed. They start out with low energy, full of suspicion, and they are often deeply introspective. With TYLA's help I have seen them become confident, outgoing team players. It is humbling to see how attention and passion can turn young people around, and to remember how few of them get this opportunity. It is not surprising that TYLA receives inquiries from around the world asking it to share the secrets of this success.

We all know how easy it is to make the wrong choices when we are young. For most of us there are family and friends to get us back on track. But what about the people who are on their own? I believe that you make a difference in this world by concentrating on one person at a time. Anyone, given the right care and attention, can realize their full potential. And I have found it to be just as true in business as it is on the streets of a city.

One of the success stories at TYLA has been the dance program offered by Auckland-based dancer Mika. I asked him how he worked with TYLA and how dance can bring new self-esteem and confidence to young people whose life is a daily struggle. You can find out more about TYLA at tyla.co.nz. KR

Intelligence versus intellect

The first thing you realize with these kids is that intelligence isn't about being able to read or write. Intelligence is quite different from intellect. Often you'll meet a very intelligent young person who just needs their mind opened up so they understand there's nothing wrong with seeing the world differently and thinking outside the box.

Around (TYLA)

I've found that in any group there are always those who want to stand out and who want to do something—kids who have a dream that is bigger than the nine-to-five. Too often young people like this keep their dreams deep inside them so they can't be damaged or taken away. The work we do at TYLA is focused on making these dreams and opportunities come alive, and the most terrific results often come from the most unlikely kids.

I remember a couple of young kids in particular who just had something special in their eyes. You could just see it. I knew that the home they went back to was a bit rough but I could see that they had a drive in them, and I knew that drive would keep them going.

Any change needs family support. Part of the selection process at TYLA is ensuring that the parents give permission and understand what is involved. Our families are such important role models that it is very difficult to make changes if there is opposition or even indifference. So for a child to break out of the cycle without *whanau* (family) support is really very hard.

Having said that, the ripples from the success of a single person can spread a long way. A positive change of attitude in one person is viral and can positively affect families, friends, and even a school. This is the way change can keep growing and create the kind of foundation that is essential if any program is to have long-term effects on individuals and in communities.

Mika—*using dance as a medium for transformation.*

Getting moving

I work for the Torotoro Trust, which is different from TYLA in some respects, but the aim is the same. My work is about getting the body moving through dance. The one thing I've learned, especially within mental health programs, is that physical activity always benefits the mind. When the mind is optimistic it tends to accept challenges, to move, develop, and change.

So my work is all about empowering young people to get up and do something. Now that might not sound like a lot, but in this age of mobile phones and fast foods it's possible for a young person to live a life that doesn't involve any physical activity at all.

The results of bringing dance into young people's lives can be spectacular. I remember one young boy who came in and to start with he didn't say "boo." Not a word. By the second week we would sometimes get a "yeah" out of him and maybe a bit of a look. You could see his eyes were starting to open, but he still wasn't saying much. By about the fourth or fifth week he was a completely different person. I'd find him coming in after school and doing his own work but also getting into some of the other things we were doing because he wanted to.

He was a fascinating example of someone who came with nothing in his mind and began to see possibilities. Seeing someone change like that makes for the most joyful moments I have in my work. From the time we first started working with him to the end of that period, he changed and became completely and utterly optimistic. He started joking and having fun every time he came in. And this was from a kid we couldn't get a word from when we first met. It was an absolute joy to see something so dramatic.

Small steps, big changes

Just getting a kid to join in might not sound like much, but for a lot of these young people to do something simple can be very, very hard. Take standing still in front of the group, saying their name without blinking or fidgeting, and walking back to their place. They can find this extremely difficult.

What is amazing though is that even learning to do something as simple as that can make a big difference to them for the rest of their lives. It means they can walk into a shop or a supermarket with confidence, without feeling they are under suspicion. These are all things you may take for granted, but for these kids they are hurdles that have to be overcome. In the end it all comes down to physical confidence and that's what we teach them.

So even though we use dance as a way to get young people into some physical activity, it's not about dance anymore. We use dance as a camouflage.

Mika with rangatahi *(young people),
Kaikohe, New Zealand.*

Buttering up a nation

Amul first came on to my radar when Arijit from India nominated it on lovemarks.com. Made by the people for the people, Amul has never lost sight of why it came into being—to give power back to Indian dairy farmers and cut out the middlemen; to create sustainable businesses that protect rural communities. Here Amul Managing Director B. M. Vyas tells us about being a business that cares, and in return is adored by the people it serves. In Lovemarks language, that's Loyalty Way Beyond Reason. KR

Why is the Indian cooperative Amul so loved? Because of the way it has connected the daily importance of dairy products—butter, milk, ghee, ice cream, and paneer—to the emotions of its consumers: Love, pride, and empowerment. Amul has become all of these things to millions of people. As India's biggest dairy cooperative, Amul is driven by a sense that it is an inseparable part of the wider community.

The Gujarat Cooperative Milk Marketing Federation (commonly known as Amul) was founded in 1946 as a beacon for the Indian cooperative movement. Since then it has been undergoing a multidimensional evolution whose overarching objective has been the same throughout: serving the farmer and catering to consumer requirements. Today 2.4 million people are members and 1.5 million gallons of milk are collected each day.

Based in Gujarat in western India, Amul helps to build opportunities and a future for farmers otherwise trapped by poverty. Amul was created by farmers for farmers. In the early 20th century dairy farmers in the region struggled to make ends meet. Few had access to proper refrigeration and in the heat, large quantities of milk quickly turned sour. Middlemen who controlled the marketing and distribution system anticipated this and paid very low prices. To defend their livelihood, the farmers created a cooperative to market their products.

However Amul is not just a source of income for its members; it touches something much deeper—the ideal effect of any good cooperative. Amul resides in the secured livelihoods of marginal farmers, in the economic and social emancipation of rural women, the education of the rural girl, the honest values delivered for the consumers' hard-earned money, and in the pride that the nation takes in its achievements.

Apart from being a source of assured employment and competitive advantage, a successful cooperative movement also instills the self-confidence and self-respect that spring from self-reliance.

A successful rural development program must also help rural people stay voluntarily and profitably in the villages. Cooperative dairy development on the Amul pattern has been instrumental in securing rural livelihoods in many parts of India, through income generation, agricultural diversification, risk distribution, female empowerment, and assured employment.

By supporting rural economies and embracing people rather than product, Amul has been crucial in building up businesses that have reversed the powerful flow of people leaving the country for the cities.

Our nation takes pride in Amul as proof that our Indian vision, backed by hard work, management skills, and honest, capable leadership, can achieve miracles.

Amul means "priceless" in Sanskrit

Members of the Gujarat Cooperative Milk Marketing Federation in various stages of the dairy production process.

UTTERLY BUTTERLY IN **LOVE!**

The Utterly Butterly girl, created by Sylvester da Cunha, has stolen the hearts of many Indian women since the first cute images were pasted around Mumbai in 1967. From their very first appearance, crowds of people were attracted to the posters and billboards around the city.

Not content to be just an icon, the Utterly Butterly girl has launched a thousand provocative and pithy advertisements on political and social issues in India.

The "Amul Moppet," in her polka dot dress and with her endearing smile, has never gone out of favor. In fact, Amul's billboard campaign is poised to take the *Guinness Book of Records* entry for the world's longest-running advertising campaign.

Amul farmers celebrate the laying of the foundation stone for a new dairy plant in Gujarat, May 2003.

Sustainable lovemarks

William McDonough

William McDonough is an architect and visionary who expresses an ecologically sound, sustainable, and revolutionary vision of environmental design. The book he co-authored, *Cradle to Cradle*, offers a view of ecological abundance that is in harmony with the environment, providing for human needs, and beyond "limits, pollution, and waste." McDonough advocates innovative design, including buildings that produce more energy than they consume, and factories that purify their own waste water.

Gill, UNITED STATES

Whole Foods

Whole Foods returns food to a fundamental celebration that moves us at the base of our being. From the brown bag lunch packed lovingly by Mom to the lavish Thanksgiving table, food is such an integral part of our lives. Other chains make food feel packaged and cheap—a mere commodity. Whole Foods reminds us why we often pair food and Love.

Karen, UNITED STATES

Bono

Bono, you are my hero without a doubt! I love your passion for helping others around the world— sometimes by writing a song, sometimes by donating directly to a good cause, sometimes by starting your own project or organization. But always with this great motivation for doing right and using your name and fame to get things done! You are a great inspiration to me—please keep up the good work!

Edgar, NETHERLANDS

Slingfings

My three Slingfings bags cheer up my life. The peg bag reminds me to smile as I hang the washing in the mornings. The beautiful carpet-style bag gets comments wherever I go during the day, and the lavender sack helps send me off into a peaceful sleep each night. The pleasure comes from looking at a beautiful object and knowing that the ethic behind the construction is ecological, loving, and passionate. An inspiration and a guide for all of us who love to create things from the world's resources without taking from it. Keep on keeping on!

Amy, UNITED KINGDOM

Muji

Simplicity. Understated elegance. Quiet, unassuming class. Muji is a brand without pretensions. Everything they make, from toothbrushes to office chairs, is designed to fulfill its purpose neatly and perfectly, and to do so without compromising the environment. Their materials are sourced globally or recycled from industrial processes. Natural colors and shapes are accentuated, not manufactured away. Muji is a perfect fusion of Love and Respect.

Catherine, CANADA

Project Daymaker

Project Daymaker has been wonderful for our agency and for people experiencing homelessness in our community. They have visited us annually for four years now. In fact, they just provided 70 haircuts in under four hours to clients of our emergency shelter last week as part of National Hunger and Homelessness Awareness Week. They always share much more than cuts, styles, and product. They add in care, compassion, dignity, respect, and a positive outlook. We love Project Daymaker and their staff!

Trudy, UNITED STATES

Put your consumers in control. Sustainable businesses address the real needs of consumers.

Remember the power of one. Give a life-changing opportunity to someone who needs it. Then give one to someone else.

Consider your local community. Find out how you can help sustain its character and articulate its dreams for the future.

Test all your business decisions against the question — will the results be sustainable?

Your business needs an inspiring purpose that people can feel emotionally committed to. Make this your personal mission.

CHAPTER EIGHT

Heartbeats

**REINVENTING RESEARCH
WITH LOVEMARKS**

Can you count the beats of my
heart? Measuring the ripples of
Lovemarks on the world stage
required market research as we
knew it to be reinvented. We had to
be counterintuitive and measure the
power of Love in the market.

Special features
Howard Roberts, Worldwide
Director of Lovemarks, Saatchi &
Saatchi

Peter Cooper, CEO, and
John Pawle, Managing Director,
QiQ International

Love bites
Toyota Corolla, United Kingdom
The New Yorker
Condé Nast "Points of Passion"
Five things to do tomorrow

My heart skipped a beat...

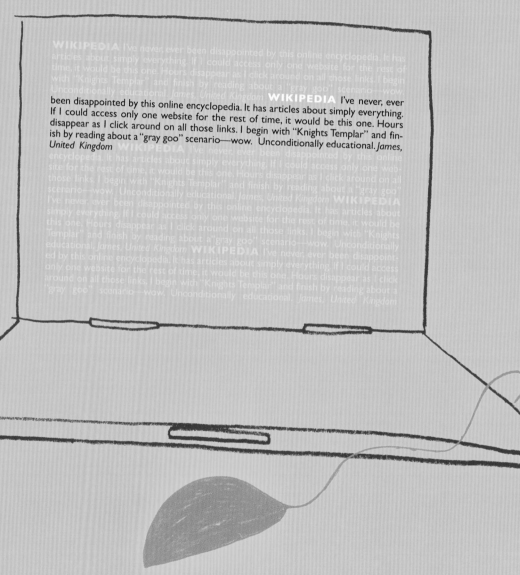

WIKIPEDIA I've never, ever been disappointed by this online encyclopedia. It has articles about simply everything. If I could access only one website for the rest of time, it would be this one. Hours disappear as I click around on all those links. I begin with "Knights Templar" and finish by reading about a "gray goo" scenario—wow. Unconditionally educational. *James, United Kingdom*

LOVEMARKS NOMINATIONS

Measuring the beats of the heart

Research has been on my mind ever since we started on the Lovemarks journey. Everything that seemed most transformative to me about Lovemarks was usually dumped in the too-hard basket by the research industry. I would put emotion and intuition on the table alongside Mystery, Sensuality, and Intimacy. I lost count of the number of times I was met by stunned silence or endless reasons why emotion couldn't be measured.

In this chapter Saatchi & Saatchi's Worldwide Director of Lovemarks, Howard Roberts, explains how the retrospective nature of the research industry made it so tough in the early days to measure what mattered about Lovemarks. He describes how we can reinvent research by including emotion, and how we can turn consumer insights into effective business foresight, action, and results.

In 2002 I spoke to an international gathering of marketing research professionals at the world research conference in Barcelona organized by ESOMAR (World Association of Research Professionals). I was direct. I said that, to me, most of the research industry felt like vampires sucking out the blood of creativity. I challenged them to count the beats of the heart rather than the fingers on their hands—to find a way to measure emotion.

This challenge was seized by Peter Cooper and John Pawle of QiQ International in London. With Saatchi & Saatchi, Peter and John developed a sophisticated model for measuring consumers' emotional responses to brands. Through their independent research, QiQ International validated the Lovemarks theory and made a major breakthrough in marrying qualitative and quantitative research in one study. Heart and head together. What we knew intuitively proved to be right in practice.

Now we can not only locate clients' brands on the Love/Respect Axis, we can connect consumers' emotions about their Lovemarks with what they buy, and create specific ways our clients' brands can start heading into Lovemarks territory. The Consumer Emotion checklist at the end of Peter and John's article will be invaluable to anyone wanting to create a Lovemark.

In this chapter we also look at Lovemarks research in action, unleashing consumer pride in the Toyota Corolla and discovering passion points for our first Lovemarks research client, *The New Yorker*. KR

Launch of the Lovemarks *book, London, England*

The emotional dimension:

Howard Roberts—*tracking the journey to Lovemarks status.*

When Neo in the film The Matrix *was asked "What is love?" he replied that love is a human emotion. He was corrected and told, "It's just a word. What matters is the connection the word implies." Today, deep and meaningful connections are being created between brands and consumers the world over. The challenge for research is to uncover and explore these connections—head and heart. Lovemarks showed us that ignoring the emotional dimension in research meant ignoring what matters most. It was time to get serious about emotion. When we appointed Howard Roberts as Saatchi & Saatchi's Worldwide Director for Lovemarks, he set to work to show that the heart rules the head.* KR

Reinventing research

Most research demands swift, cost-effective, clear answers and results that can be compared over time. Research is fundamentally used to justify marketing activities retroactively. Businesses feel safer with data and charts that give some sense to the chaos of the market.

Research and marketing seem to be obsessed with understanding and plotting "the consumer," the behavior of the consumer, with consumers depicted as logical, decisive individuals making sensible, considered decisions about their purchases. Their processes of consumption are treated in isolation without considering emotion.

Lovemarks theory challenges this model. It treats consumers as emotionally-driven beings who usually apply conscious scrutiny to their decisions only after the event. It also reveals that their behaviors are highly relationship-based, with the relevant emotions at hand.

Research has to adapt to embrace this alternative view of how consumers operate. Researchers have to stop measuring what is easy to measure, and grapple with the powerful drivers of behavior that lie beneath the surface and are tough to get a numerical grip on.

Engaging the emotions

Tina Turner asked, "What's love got to do with it, what's love but a second-hand emotion?" That's one way of looking at it, but it ignores what we know instinctively: that human beings are emotional creatures. How did we go

Lovemarks research

about convincing our heads that this is so? What follows is some of the thinking that developed as we dug deep into emotional research, realizing that for the first time, Lovemarks could help us to get a handle on the deeper relationships that exist between consumers and brands.

1. WE HAVE TO GO DEEPER THAN RATIONALITY

Psychological theory and common sense converge to tell us that each and every purchase decision cannot be the product of separate, rational judgments reached after analysis of the evidence.

Take buying a coffee, for example. In the average Starbucks, there is a dazzling choice of around 6,000 coffee combinations. If you made a conscious decision to try a different one every day, it would take you more than 16 years to drink your way through the menu.

2. WE HAVE TO BRING THE SUBCONSCIOUS TO THE SURFACE

Neuroscience has it that only 5 percent of brain activity is conscious, and as a consequence nearly all consumer decision-making has to be sub-conscious, or takes place as a low-level process. Professor Reed Montague (Director of the Brown Foundation Human Neuroimaging Laboratory at Baylor) observed that when confronted with brand choice, there is a response in the brain that leads to a behavioural effect. This activity in the brain is related to the control of actions, the dredging up of memories and self-image. And curiously, it has nothing to do with conscious preference.

3. WE HAVE TO PUT REASON AND EMOTION TOGETHER

The brain works in two ways to integrate emotions and reasoning in decision-making. The first is when the rational part of the brain, the prefrontal cortex, sends messages to the decision centers and we behave in a rational, considered manner. This is far less common than we would like to believe.

The second way the brain works is far more common and much more interesting. Here the messages come from the sensory part of the brain, the sensory cortex. They override the rational processes and we behave in

> ❝ Working with Lovemarks we have found that the most penetrating question for clients is not whether they are a Lovemark, but how they are faring on the journey towards Lovemark status. ❞
>
> HOWARD ROBERTS

an impulsive, instinctive manner. Joseph Ledoux, Professor of Neuroscience at New York University observed that, "The connections from the emotional systems to the rational cognitive systems are stronger than the connections that run the other way."

The development of Lovemarks research

Consumer decision-making driven by intuition, instinct, and emotion is difficult enough for qualitative research techniques to grasp, but to standard quantitative techniques it is clearly alien territory. The challenge was to evolve quantitative research so that it could measure the seemingly immeasurable—the heartfelt bonds between people and brands.

In the case of Lovemarks this meant finding a way to measure not just Love and Respect, but to explore the variety of relationships that existed, examine the key drivers of Mystery, Sensuality, and Intimacy, and tie them to rigorous business results.

Over 18 months QiQ International developed and validated such a research tool. It is now possible to measure Lovemarks. It is possible to build a model of how the measures might be applied to any specific brand, and to demonstrate the return on investment for doing so. The results are enlightening and unequivocal. They are described by Peter Cooper and John Pawle in their article "Measuring Emotion and the Validation of Lovemarks" that follows.

Working with Lovemarks we have found that the most penetrating question for clients is not whether they are a Lovemark, but how they are faring on the journey towards Lovemark status. To help us navigate brands on this journey we have developed a suite of innovative research products that deal with the need for both qualitative and quantitative insights, data, and knowledge.

Today's learning will shape tomorrow

From the work we have done so far we can draw three important insights:

1. People bring their own context and values to Lovemarks. The principle that consumers own Lovemarks is fundamental. Brands only exist in people's heads, so it is *their* idea of what a brand is that matters, not ours. Our job is to understand this, and work with it. If we can explore people's own realities rather than trying to make them understand things they will never believe, then we can move brands forward.

2. People have no hesitation about using the "L-word" to express their feelings towards products and services. Although as marketers we have always shied away from using "love," consumers have no such reluctance. They use the word love with ease, and they mean it.

3. The importance of stories. Telling a single story can explain a life-long commitment, and people have been happy to tell their love stories (and their hate stories!) in droves. Stories do not only tap into the power of curiosity, but provide us with a powerful resource for study and insights.

Lovemarks research continues to develop as we partner with psychologists, anthropologists, and neuroscientists to explore new insights into people, and the depth and complexity of their relationships with, and feelings towards, brands.

There's plenty to uncover. As novelist Maya Angelou observed, "People will forget what you said, people will forget what you did, but people will never forget how you made them feel."

HEART OVER HEAD IN LOVE WITH COROLLA

How do you take a car that has been described as something that says "absolutely nothing about you" and turn it into a Lovemark? This was the challenge presented in the United Kingdom by the Toyota Corolla. The problem was that consumers were not "seeing" the Corolla, even when it was right in front of them. This was a car that was being taken for granted, a car that needed to get in touch with consumer feelings. Howard Roberts tells the story of how car-buyers fell in love. KR

THE CHALLENGE

The Corolla is a great car. Technically superior to its competition, the Corolla is the world's best-selling automobile, a world rally car champion, and has topped the J D Power and Associates customer satisfaction index for five years.

Yet for all these great qualities, the Corolla was a brand tagged as bland. The general opinion? "The

Toyota Corolla is the ideal car for every undercover agent—it says absolutely nothing about you."

In terms of image the Corolla fell far behind its two main rivals—the VW Golf and the Ford Focus. The Golf was a highly aspirational, emotional purchase and the gold standard in its class. This was the car to which all others were compared—people simply wanted to be seen in them. The Focus was the default option, seen as the best all-round car and the benchmark in engineering and design.

The Corolla was between a rock and a hard place, with buyers purchasing because of the attractive price and the vehicle's dependability. But it was not a car to brag about.

The Lovemark challenge was to create the Corolla as a heart over head purchase. To inspire those who would never think of purchasing a Corolla, not just to consider one, but to desire one.

PRIDE IN THE NAME OF LOVE

A group of smart 30-somethings gave the key insight. These people were intensely proud of their possessions and their achievements. This sense of pride inspired the creative idea: the lengths people will go to in order to associate themselves with a Corolla. The emotion we were looking for was clear: Pride.

Pride is about confidence. It means you can be assertive, and sometimes it means you let the heart overrule the head. These were the emotions the Corolla wanted to touch.

Pride can't simply be justified. You have to get out there and claim it. As soon as you listed "reasons why you should be proud of the Corolla," the idea was rejected, as was the car. Assertion, not justification, had to be the tone. Corolla *is* a car to be proud of. End of story.

The campaign wittily put the Corolla in situations that proved someone really, really loved this car. And they were prepared to demonstrate their pride anywhere. On television and radio as well as street posters and signs, drive-in movies, and health club promotions.

"Proud owner" became an understatement.

The results?

It's no overstatement to say the idea completely transformed Corolla's position. In image terms, Corolla shifted from "dull and boring" to "a car to be seen in." On the back of this idea, Corolla moved up from seventh to second in the United Kingdom car market, and achieved its highest-ever share. Fifty percent more cars were sold, at a 20 percent higher price.

Is the Corolla a Lovemark? Ask a Corolla owner.

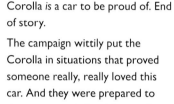

A car to attract envious glances from my peers

KNOWN FOR THINGS THAT I CARE ABOUT

KNOWN FOR THINGS THAT ARE DIFFERENT

Reliable, good value, with plenty of equipment, but dull and driven by old people

KNOWN FOR SOMETHING

KNOWN FOR GOOD THINGS

KNOWN

UNKNOWN

COROLLA'S JOURNEY
The goal was to take the Corolla from "known for something" to "known for things people care about."

HAVE YOU SEEN THIS CAR?

NICE ISN'T IT?

Phone Phil on 0845 275 5555

Measuring emotion and the validation of Lovemarks

When Peter Cooper and John Pawle of QiQ International took up my challenge at ESOMAR, they started a fascinating journey with Saatchi & Saatchi. QiQ International have investigated Lovemarks theory by finding new ways to measure emotion, to measure Mystery, Sensuality, and Intimacy, and to measure Love and Respect—and to tie them all into measurable business results. The most significant finding? "There is conclusive evidence that creating a Lovemark will increase sales." Saatchi & Saatchi and QiQ International have now completed several Lovemarks research studies and have many more in progress with clients in industries ranging from consumer finance to pharmaceuticals, packaged goods to beverages. John and Peter have also had a paper on Lovemarks published in the Journal of Advertising Research *in March 2006 called "Measuring Emotion: Lovemarks, the future beyond brands." They prepared the following paper to set out how they have validated the idea of Lovemarks.* KR

The Lovemarks research challenge

To create a Lovemark, marketing strategy needs to focus on increasing Love and Respect for a brand by maximizing the consumer's emotional connection with it. Our research focused on diagnosing how to achieve these emotional connections by obtaining an in-depth understanding of the brand-person relationship.

QUALITATIVE AND QUANTITATIVE TECHNIQUES

Conventional research separates qualitative and quantitative approaches: qualitative for assessing emotion in-depth or in groups and quantitative for measuring behavior and surface attitudes in questionnaires. To measure Lovemarks we combined implicit, emotional, and unconscious effects with explicit, conscious, rational effects, and produced metrics for both.

Specific evidence in favor of a radically holistic approach comes from contemporary neuroscience, which demonstrates that the brain itself functions holistically, and that emotions play a previously unrecognized part in determining behavior. Neuropsychologist Antonio Damasio states that "over 85 percent of thought, emotions, and learning occur in the unconscious mind."

BETA TESTING OF LOVEMARKS

In 2003 we undertook the beta testing of Lovemarks theory based on our techniques. The sample was drawn from a panel with a US membership of 175,000. Three hundred respondents were selected to explore different aspects of car and food categories.

The main objectives for the tests were:

- to establish for what proportion of users the brand being measured was a Lovemark;

- to estimate the increase in sales volume when the number of users for whom the brand is a Lovemark increased;

- to provide insight into critical dimensions on which the brand needs to strengthen the brand-person relationship.

The beta test fieldwork was conducted entirely online. Our experience shows that computer self-completion interviewing has many advantages. Without an interviewer present, respondents feel more spontaneous, honest, and willing to explore sensitive issues. The Lovemark measures of emotion are adapted from qualitative in-depth techniques including word and picture associations, guided dreams, and "bubble" pictures. These work well with an interactive computer interface and give us rich detail through open-ended responses.

Peter Cooper *(top) and* ***John Pawle*** *(bottom)—putting numbers to emotion.*

THE PATHWAYS MODEL

We developed the Pathways Model for understanding and measuring the role of emotion in brand-person relationships.[1] The model demonstrates how brand messages are routed through a rational pathway and an emotional pathway, and shows how they are integrated through the "executive function" of the ego.

From this model the current brand-person relationship can be defined along with specific emotions that depend on socio-cultural codes. The methods we have described for understanding the process and which

THE PATHWAYS MODEL

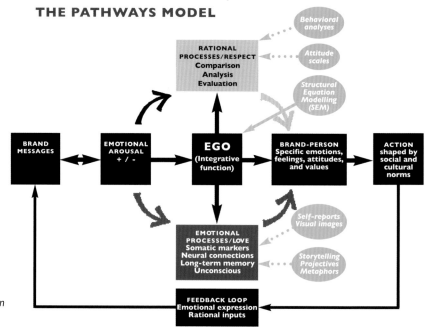

Fig.1 QiQ International, 2005

How brand messages are routed through a rational pathway and an emotional pathway.

mechanisms they tap are shown in Fig.1. They are brought together in the analysis of the brand relationship and current consumer action.

The output is the market research feeding back into the brand, indicating which emotional and rational factors need to be increased, and which factors need to be reduced, to enhance the brand relationship.

In measuring the emotional processes shown in the Pathways Model, we take two routes. First we ask respondents for emotional and visual associations with each brand being tested. These are fed into our structural equation model that tracks what is happening in the "executive function" of the ego. Secondly, we use projective techniques for a psychological analysis of what is driving the brand's equity.

MEASURING THE BRAND-PERSON RELATIONSHIP

Respondents first need to entertain the idea that brands are like people. Some people you are passionate about while you are indifferent to others. The relationship types we use are similar to those described by Susan Fournier.[2]

Respondents are asked to sort brands into the relationship categories and to rate the Respect they have for each brand. Visual association is then used to further diagnose the nature of the relationship. This generates a position for each brand on the "Love/Respect Axis" (see Fig.2).

LOVE/RESPECT AXIS

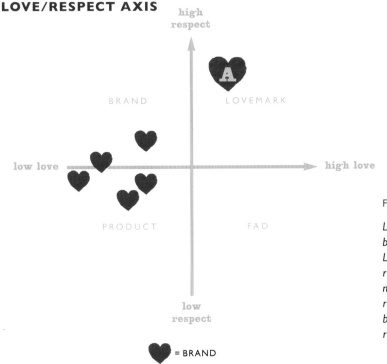

Fig.2 QiQ International, 2005

Locations generated in the food category beta test clearly show that Brand A is a Lovemark because it is strongly loved and respected. Most other contenders in this market remain brands because they are respected but not yet loved, or products because they are neither strongly loved nor respected.

THE FACTORS THAT TRANSFORM A BRAND INTO A LOVEMARK

Current concepts of brands pay careful attention to the rational and symbolic aspects of brands, but often overlook their sensory, experiential, or synaesthetic aspects.[3] After Intimacy and Mystery, Sensuality is critical in building a passionate relationship. All five senses influence how brands are perceived.

We use association techniques and guided dreams as powerful creative techniques that can be quantified. The analysis of the brand-person dialogue provides powerful insights into both left brain (cognition) and right brain (feelings). Storytelling is a fundamental means by which consumers make sense of the world. It is also integral to Lovemarks theory.

NETWORK OF INFLUENCES ON LOVE AND RESPECT

Fig.3 QiQ International, 2005

The degree of correlation between the factors of Love and Respect in the food category beta test indicates the order of influence. Line thickness shows the strength of a correlation. Where there is no line between factors there is a negligible correlation.

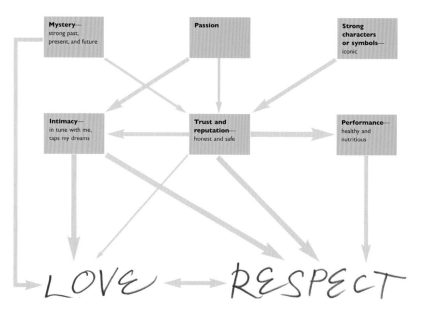

Psychologist David Schiffrin writes, "We dream in narrative, daydream in narrative, remember, anticipate, hope, despair, believe, doubt, plan, revise, criticize, gossip, learn, hate, and love by narrative."[4]

We find that stories are major ways in which Lovemarks resonate with people's everyday lives. Consumer stories about Lovemarks are often several hundred words long, indicating their rich and guiding roles.

We use the skills and intuition of professional psychologists to diagnose our various interactive techniques. They produce a set of analyses based upon small subsets, which are then coded and quantified by trained analysts. For example, psychologists diagnose storytelling using archetypal story analysis (ASA) to identify brand archetypes.[5]

INTEGRATING THE EMOTIONAL AND FUNCTIONAL

Lovemarks research identifies functional processes mainly through rating scales. These determine how hot, warm, or cold respondents feel about brands in terms of trust, respect, performance, and category-specific attributes. We also include conventional behavioral questions on buying habits and future propensity to purchase. This data allows us to explore how emotional processes link to functional processes as set out in the Pathways Model (Fig.1).

The next stage is to show how these influences interact. Structural Equation Modeling (SEM) draws inferences about emotion from statistical analyses of verbal and nonverbal rating scales, and verbal and visual brand association techniques. SEM can be used to identify the quantitative contribution of functional and emotional factors, and to examine the effects of modifying components of each in "What if...?" creative scenario planning.

This analysis results in a description of the web of bonds that underpins the person-brand relationship. Typically, the main factors that drive Love for a brand are purely emotional, whereas the factors driving Respect are more functional, performance-related attributes.

34% Intimacy—
in tune with my dreams

28% Mystery—
strong past, present, and future

14% Strong characters or symbols—
iconic

10% Trust and reputation—
honest and safe

9% Passion

5% Performance—
healthy and nutritious

Fig.4 QiQ International, 2005

Percentages reflect the weight of each element in the total relationship in the food category beta test.

Our analysis shows that the dominant factors are Intimacy and Mystery, which influence both Love and Respect, and Trust, which mainly influences Respect. Intimacy is how closely in tune a respondent feels with the brand, how relevant and empathetic it is to them. Mystery also plays a part in influencing Love, and strong characters and symbols influence Trust.

Two functional factors, Trust (reputation, honest, and safe) and Performance (healthy and nutritious), influenced Respect in the food category beta test. But as noted, Respect is also influenced by Intimacy.

Intimacy is invariably the most important influence on purchasing across all categories we have measured. Intimacy is, of course, highly emotional, and is in turn driven by another emotional factor: passion. Subsequent research has shown that passion is often a strong element of Intimacy or, as in this case, a strong underlying factor.

THE VALIDATION OF LOVEMARKS

Other Lovemarks research studies carried out across many different categories confirm the contention of Lovemarks that the key factors that influence Love are Intimacy, Mystery, and then Sensuality, and the key factors that influence Respect are Trust, Reputation, and Performance.

The major deviation from Lovemarks theory shown by the research is that consumers do not normally see Love and Respect as separate factors. They are correlated to various degrees according to the product category. The specific contribution of Love and Respect factors varies as we investigate more categories.

The Sensuality of a brand is worth noting. It is often a key factor as measured by the images it creates in consumers' minds—sounds, music, texture, colors, tastes, and smells: the total sensory experience. Sensuality tends to have a direct influence on Intimacy and hence on Love.

THE INFLUENCE OF EMOTIONAL AND FUNCTIONAL FACTORS ON BRAND-PERSON RELATIONSHIPS

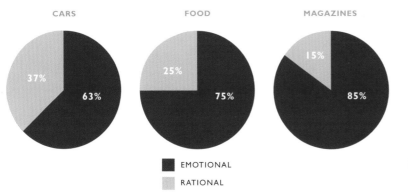

CARS FOOD MAGAZINES

■ EMOTIONAL
▨ RATIONAL

Fig.5 QiQ International, 2005

THE POWER OF EMOTION

Using multiple regression we can estimate the degree of influence of emotion. Fig 5 shows the extent to which emotional factors influence the closeness of the relationship. We can also see the degree of influence on rational factors, for the three beta-test studies.

This is strong evidence that the relationships people have with brands are much more heavily influenced by emotional than by rational factors. Our impression is that rational factors mainly help to justify decisions driven by emotions.

THE IMPACT OF EMOTION ON BRAND VOLUME

Does building Love and Respect for a brand increase its sales volume? Making this connection was a vital role of our beta test of the Lovemarks theory. From the following example and many others, our work has made this critical connection.

In the examples in Fig.6 and Fig.7, Lovemark consumers are between four and seven times more likely to purchase a Lovemark than a product, and between 1.6 and 2.3 times more likely to purchase a Lovemark than a brand. This effectively means that moving a brand from being highly respected to a Lovemark position, where it is both loved and highly respected, can double volume.

RESULT OF BEING A LOVEMARK
Fig.6 and Fig.7 QiQ International, 2005

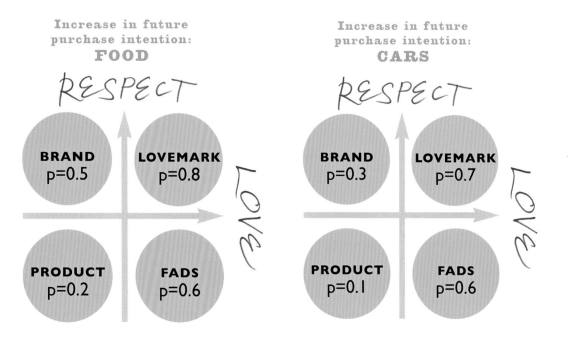

p= increase in future purchase intention

OVERALL CONCLUSIONS

- Intimacy, Mystery, and Sensuality as well as Trust, Reputation, and Performance do exist and, furthermore, they emerge from multivariate analysis as the main influences on Love and Respect for brands. The factors that most influence buying intention are the emotional factors that drive Love—in particular Intimacy, followed closely by Mystery, and underpinned by Sensuality.

- Consistently, the key emotional triggers in strengthening the brand-person relationship and creating brand intimacy are, across different product categories, the need to make the brand highly relevant and to invite consumers to feel more closely in tune with and passionate about a brand.

- The second most important factor is Mystery, which means the brand must tap consumer dreams by being iconic and having great stories associated with it.

- Sensuality, although less of a direct influence on buying intention, is a strong trigger for closer Intimacy and a stronger sense of Mystery. Sensuality is about creating a richer and fuller brand experience by developing brands that touch all the senses.

- There is conclusive evidence that creating a Lovemark will increase sales. Growing Love and Respect can increase buying intention by as much as seven times. Once a product has built Respect and thus become a brand, it can increase its volume by up to two times by increasing Love and becoming a Lovemark.

CONSUMER EMOTION CHECKLIST

Ten key insights about emotion to aid understanding of the consumer's response to marketing

1. Brand emotions are felt mental and/or physical experiences of arousal directed towards changing consumer behavior, or if not behavior, changing a view, value, disposition, or attitude towards a brand.

2. Brand emotions and the feelings associated with them originate from the brand and its total communications. Over time they can also arise from long-term memory images and associations via neural connections in the brain known as somatic markers.

3. Brand emotions can be personal, private, and difficult to articulate. They are communicated through words, behavior, body language, and metaphors for the emotional experience.

4. There are certain basic and universal emotions, but emotional expression is subtle and highly variable. Expression is also dependent on cultural context, and needs interpretation to understand local nuances.

5. Brand emotions generate conscious feelings and rational judgments, but there are typically unconscious connections, too, that play major parts in brand relationships and behavior. To obtain the full picture they need to be identified by projective methods.

6. The way people express emotions in an interview is subject to social rules about what is appropriate or not. This can distort actual feelings. The most effective method is interviewing that is free of prejudice or influence, making computer self-completion a useful technique.

7. Although there are an almost infinite number of shades of feelings, for practical purposes emotions are limited to those which are conventionally coded and understood in everyday life.

8. There are two pathways in response to the emotional stimuli in brand communication: one cognitive, the other emotional. These are integrated via an "ego executive function" which seeks to optimize a person's satisfaction in the context of personal, social, and cultural values.

9. Emotional responses to brands, purchasing, and consumption in modern life are also the result of increasing pressure on time, brand differentiation, and attention. Emotionally-based brand decisions are increasing as a result of these pressures, while cognitive functions are often on "auto-pilot" to simplify decisions. This trend, however, is responsive to the economic development of a market.

10. Emotional pathways in many product fields are usually rapid and impulsive. They bypass the cognitive functions of rational judgment and lead to direct action. The role of rationality is to justify decisions—often in the eyes of other people.

References

C. Booker, 2004, *The Seven Basic Plots*, London: Continuum International Publishing Group.

P. Cooper and A. Branthwaite, 2002, *Synaesthesia: Researching the Power of Sensation*, Boston: Proceedings of the ESOMAR Worldwide Qualitative Research Conference.

P. Cooper and J. Pawle, 2002, *Horse and Carriage, Moonlight and Roses, Sun and Surf?*, Los Angeles: Proceedings of the ESOMAR AFR World Audience Measurement Conference.

P. Cooper and J. Pawle, 2005, *Measuring Emotion in Brand Communication*, Paris: ESOMAR Innovate Conference.

A. Damasio, 1999, *The Feeling of What Happens: Body and Emotion in the Making of Consciousness*, New York: Harcourt Brace and Co.

S.M. Fournier, 1998, *Consumers and Their Brands: Developing Relationship Theory in Consumer Research*, Journal of Consumer Research (Issue 24).

W. Gordon, 2001, *The Darkroom of the Mind—What Does Neuropsychology Now Tell Us About Brands?*, Journal of Consumer Behavior (Vol.1, No.3)

K. Roberts, 2002, *Stop! In the Name of Love*, Barcelona: ESOMAR 2002 Congress.

K. Roberts, 2004, *Lovemarks: the future beyond brands*, New York: powerHouse Books.

D. Schiffrin, 1996, *Narrative as Self-Portrait: Sociolinguistic Constructions of Identity*, Language in Society (Issue 25).

1. Cooper and Pawle, 2005
2. Fournier, 1998
3. Cooper and Branthwaite, 2002
4. Schiffrin, 1996
5. Booker, 2004

THE NEW YORKER

Imagine my delight when in January 2004 my favorite magazine, *The New Yorker*, agreed to become QiQ International's first commercial client on a Lovemarks research project. Could there be a better Lovemark to explore the power of the methodology?

The New Yorker was first published in 1925 and over the decades has continued to be serious, funny, intelligent, penetrating, and relevant. Editor David Remnick describes *The New Yorker* as a collection of human voices, and this insight reveals much of the magazine's long-lived appeal.

Considered intuitively, *The New Yorker* tracks high on many Lovemarks characteristics, such as great stories and icons, inspiration, and empathy. The publishers wanted to get beyond intuition, however, to prove to their advertisers that *The New Yorker*

was special, and to explain why. In short, they wanted to identify the value of their Lovemark status. Their goal was to understand more about their readers and to develop insights which would help differentiate *The New Yorker*, reinforce the loyalty of subscribers, and attract new readers. Finally, they wanted to compare *The New Yorker* with key competitive media.

QiQ International conducted online research using its proprietary Lovemarks question bank and storytelling methodology. The sample was split between 300 *New Yorker* readers, half of them subscribers. Both samples were representative of the reader profile.

The results were outstanding and clearly demonstrated that *The New Yorker* was a Lovemark to its subscribers. In fact the figures showed that subscribers read *The New Yorker* with 15 times the

amount of Love and five times the Respect they applied to competitive titles. This result put *The New Yorker* into Lovemarks' top right-hand quadrant of the Love/Respect Axis and competitive titles into the brand or commodity quadrants.

The value of being a Lovemark was beyond dispute. *The New Yorker*'s Lovemarks status drives reading frequency. In media, the shift from brand to Lovemark increases readership by 155 percent.

A further useful finding was the fact that *The New Yorker* has a stronger "emotional halo" than its competition. Readers of other titles do not have the same intensity of relationship. This makes *The New Yorker* a unique medium with positive benefits for advertisers and other partners. KR

It's not a subscription, it's a torrid love affair.

There's a connection
our readers have
with our magazines.
A connection
fueled by passion.

© 2006 The Condé Nast Publications, Inc.

p.s. Let's get passionate

Condé Nast Publications creates great magazines like The New Yorker, Vanity Fair, and Vogue. Each of their titles share one important quality: passion. It is a passion for ideas, for images, for design, and for people. Condé Nast titles have intense empathy with their readers, who are deeply committed in return. Recently Condé Nast put this two-way relationship at the heart of an impressive print campaign by Heat of San Francisco. They called the series "Point of Passion." KR

CONDÉ NAST
MEDIA GROUP

THE POINT OF PASSION.

Evaluate the balance of emotional and rational factors in your brand. Which ones make the most difference?

Nominate yourself as Chief Feedback Fan. Dream up new ways to invite consumers to talk back. Take them seriously.

Look at how you measure success in your business. Transform your metrics with Mystery, Sensuality, and Intimacy.

Talk to everyone. Cab drivers, waiters, neighbors, colleagues. Great researchers have great empathy and insatiable curiosity.

Lurk and listen. Real world observation nourishes great ideas.

CHAPTER NINE

Love goes to work

SAATCHI & SAATCHI CREATING LOVEMARKS

Saatchi & Saatchi people use Lovemarks to inspire, create, and innovate. Eight of Saatchi & Saatchi's ideas people share their insights for creating emotional connections and bringing Lovemarks to life in the world.

Special feature
Saatchi & Saatchi Forum

Love bites
Lights, camera, love—Lovemarks at work
Five things to do tomorrow

a golden moment

PILSNER URQUELL BEER Pilsner Urquell was the first golden beer. Urquell is the German word for "source." This source was a new strain of hops stolen from Bavarian monks and smuggled out of Germany. They produced a beer that was golden, clear, and pure—very unlike the dark and cloudy beers of old. The creation of the golden beer coincided with the practice of drinking beer from glasses rather than from earthenware tankards as before. For the first time people could see the beer they were drinking and it was beautiful. *Irina Gorshkova, Saatchi & Saatchi Russia*

Being a Lovemarks Company

Talking Lovemarks is one thing, but creating them and living the Lovemarks dream is something else again. How do you create Loyalty Beyond Reason? Where does the power of ideas lie? How can Mystery, Sensuality, and Intimacy continue to make emotional connections with consumers in the long term? Where do theory and practice meet?

The steps, as we have already seen, are deceptively simple. Build on Respect, infuse your brand with Mystery, Sensuality, and Intimacy, and develop a Lovemarks community. All this of course relies on the conviction that the consumer owns the brand. Giving this power away can form intense emotional relationships with consumers. The new consumer is always on the lookout for companies that really understand what she is about. She wants them to make decisions based on a deep understanding of who she is and her aspirations.

By using Lovemarks in our own business, we have been able to create stories and images that are both emotionally compelling and memorable.

For our clients the introduction of Mystery, Sensuality, and Intimacy creates the opportunity to form intensely emotional connections with their consumers. Clients have also been quick to understand the direct relationship between Lovemarks and growth in the market.

In this chapter a group of Lovemarks advocates from our business bring their own personal and insightful responses to the evolution of Lovemarks. They talk about how they have worked with Lovemarks in their own markets and with their own people, based in China, Costa Rica, Hong Kong, India, Italy, Russia, and Switzerland.

Here also is a selection of recent campaigns where Lovemarks thinking can be seen hard at work. From the stunning photography for the Whale and Dolphin Conservation Society campaign to the moving and socially constructive Guinness "Poem," Lovemarks inspire ideas, insights, and images. KR

Beating Heart-China

Launch of Lovemarks, *Beijing, China.*

SAATCHI & SAATCHI FORUM

Pully Chau
CEO, Saatchi & Saatchi China

V. Shantakumar
Managing Director and CEO, Saatchi & Saatchi India

Jane Wagner
CEO, Saatchi & Saatchi Russia

Anthony Plant
CEO, Saatchi & Saatchi Hong Kong

Pedro Simko
CEO, Saatchi & Saatchi Simko Switzerland

Carol Miller Repetto
EVP, Global Equity Director, Saatchi & Saatchi Italy

John Bowman
EVP, Executive Group Planning Director, Saatchi & Saatchi New York

Jorge Oller
President, Tribu/Nazca Saatchi & Saatchi Costa Rica

What do you mean when you talk about being an Ideas Company?

CAROL MILLER REPETTO Ideas get us beyond "selling by yelling." That's the old model, which operated without a trace of a consumer insight. In essence, the difference between an advertising agency and an Ideas Company is that an Ideas Company recognizes that people operate on heart, soul, and emotion, and that to really connect with people you need strong vehicles that will convey the essence of your brands. That's the definition of a great idea. It conveys the heart and soul of your brand—unlocked through your consumer insights—and makes a real emotional connection.

That's why we always start with consumer insights. But you don't get to really interesting insights by just sitting listening to a focus group. You have to get out there, where people live and play, and go about your insight gathering in much more inventive ways. My experience is that you can't do authentic marketing if it doesn't come out of authentic consumer experiences. You will only touch on authentic experiences if you get close to what matters to consumers. When you're searching for heart and soul, that's where you'll find it. That's when you hit the mark.

JANE WAGNER We opened Saatchi & Saatchi Russia as an Ideas Company in September 2004. I often think we get a bit carried away trying to define what an idea is. So many of our big ideas come from intuition and gut feelings. In the end a great idea needs to either solve a problem or understand an opportunity. The benefit is the potential to create Lovemarks.

When I'm searching for ideas I always look at kids for inspiration. Kids are great—when they are bored they always have an idea like "let's go dam the stream," or "let's go build a hideout." It got me thinking that an idea is basically a simple yet insightful collection of words based on a universal truth and need. Our work as an Ideas Company means solving a strategic opportunity using something that inspires us to transform or create Lovemark communications, and lead people to action. These big ideas are based on a human truth, something we can all identify with.

PULLY CHAU I agree. A big idea should leverage on powerful, locally relevant emotions, ones that overcome multiple barriers.

佳洁士

健康自信 笑容传中国

Crest "Keeps China Smiling Confidently"
billboard at Guangzhou Airport, China.

V. SHANTAKUMAR For an Ideas Company, an idea is something that can be executed in myriad ways without losing its essence. Nothing is sacred except the idea itself, and the idea must be the embodiment of a simple truth that connects in a way that goes straight to the heart. That is why great ideas don't need selling—they are already in the heart of the receiver. What they are expressing is an external reflection of something that is already there.

In India we have taken an idea called "god" and, for the last 4,000 to 5,000 years, have managed to keep it alive in the most amazing fashion. At the last count we had more than 100,000 gods and goddesses. Each is a Lovemark for a particular group of people—with total Loyalty Beyond Reason. This situation has been sustained through changing times, rules, and technologies. We have found, as life gets faster and more complex, it is an idea that grows stronger and the loyalty just gets fiercer.

JORGE OLLER Yes, and we shouldn't forget that ideas can create emotions of all types: empathy, melancholy, anger, attraction, envy, jealousy, closeness, and of course love. That's why so many great ideas feel like something that has always been within us: something so obvious you can't believe it had never been thought of before. Perhaps all great ideas exist in our collective unconscious and are just waiting to be expressed.

ANTHONY PLANT A powerful idea captures our imagination. It is at once inspirational and mind-expanding, and leaves us feeling richer for its brilliance. We've found that while Trustmarks perform at the product level, Lovemarks, through harnessing the true power of ideas, connect at a human level—making ideas an integral part of the Lovemarks journey.

This has certainly been our experience in China with Crest Toothpaste. To challenge for leadership, Crest needed to transcend the concept of "fresher, whiter, healthier" and offer the Chinese people something on a grander, more emotional scale. The campaign idea that captured this for Crest was "Keeps China smiling confidently." We have seen the power of this idea build an emotional connection between Crest and the confidence and healthy smile of the new China. Over nine years, Crest climbed from an unknown to one of China's biggest brands. In 2005 Crest leads the market with 30 percent share. That's the power of ideas, right there.

What is the role of emotion in the process of transformation?

PEDRO SIMKO That's a great story. It's simple stories like that, stories that everyone can relate to, that make it easy to understand how Lovemarks operate. They also transform Lovemarks from a marketing theory into a universal truth. That's why we have no difficulty at all convincing our clients that Lovemarks work.

PULLY CHAU Five years ago, after 15 years of exposure in China, Olay was becoming a mothers' brand. Young women, as they earned higher salaries, were talking about moving to other brands. It was a big alarm signal. So we consciously made Olay younger and more premium-positioned, to stay ahead of Chinese consumers. To do this we explored the powerful idea of "Love the skin you're in." But it just wasn't enough.

Emotionally, Chinese women are progressive, and expect anything they buy to transform them in some way. To respond to this we evolved the campaign idea "Amazement starts from skin." The transformation promised in commercials is not just skin-deep but life-changing. For example, the assertive designer working in cosmopolitan Shanghai imagines herself winning awards on the international stage. The housewife in a small city is promised romance. Junior secretaries dream of a discovery and trips overseas.

Olay "Total Effects" print advertisement, China.

The result? In 2003 and 2004 Olay became a Lovemark for older *and* younger women. It was loved by both mothers and daughters! And this happened in spite of the fact that we have never shown a "mature" woman on screen. In Asia even a 70-year-old woman will admire a 17-year-old girl. I can't imagine any Asian woman saying that the model is "too beautiful or unreal." Being youthful, beautiful, and having perfect skin and a great life are the biggest motivations for buying Olay.

We have found that when consumers fall in love with a brand, they constantly look out for new surprises and things that will amaze them. As with the magic in a courtship, a Lovemark must continue to surprise.

Saatchi & Saatchi Russia.

JANE WAGNER In Russia, the first transformation we had to undertake when we joined Saatchi & Saatchi was to step up from being a young agency and embrace the idea of Lovemarks. We literally had to transform the way we worked and thought as an agency, and we achieved this through our use of the power of emotion. What counted most was our positive attitude and our belief that nothing is impossible. Without Lovemarks as our central philosophy we would not have achieved any of the transformations we have witnessed and lived to date. For us Lovemarks is a new way of talking to clients, staff, and consumers, and by constantly talking the talk and walking the walk we have managed to transform our relationships with our clients.

Clients cannot resist the idea of Loyalty Beyond Reason. Even our most conservative client said to us, "We have to have this." It appeals to their sense of love, it's the ultimate seduction. When one is in love one has loads of fun. As Confucius says, "Choose a job you love, and you will never have to work a day in your life." We try to infuse this into the spirit of Russia's Ideas Company.

CAROL MILLER REPETTO I have found that because emotions are so central to people's lives the suggestion of using them in marketing has a powerful effect on clients. Emotions are easily absorbed and understood by all, and they create lasting and meaningful brand connections with consumers. While it is true that some clients initially struggle with this idea, it is a simple matter to show them how easy it is to go from an emotional low to an emotional high.

I have done this by simply showing them how quickly their eyes can fill with tears just by watching a short movie clip, and how five seconds later they can be rocking with laughter. When I am with clients I like to introduce emotions on this very human level. Finally, I ask them to imagine how their brand would grow and prosper if we could have consumers associate it with such powerful emotional responses.

ANTHONY PLANT We had this experience with consumers in Indonesia. Our work with Aqua, a bottled water company, helped them become number one in this country.

In Indonesia, the only way consumers classify drinking waters is on the basis of safety—"Is this water safe enough to drink or not?" If water is safe to drink, only then is it good enough for me and my family. It is all about Respect. There are water refilling stations in Indonesia offering water that is safe to drink at half the cost of bottled water, but many consumers are not happy with the idea of water as a basic commodity. We found that many people appreciated the essential elemental nature of water and that they wanted a relationship with drinking water that went beyond the functional. By understanding this emotional desire we were able to present Aqua as more than just drinking water. The line we used was, "Drink the best water, and you'll get the best out of life itself." Today Aqua water has the highest top-of-mind brand awareness of any beverage in Indonesia. That's not just water. Any beverage! In Indonesia, in any seven day period, 84 percent of water consumers purchase Aqua.

JORGE OLLER There is no better way to put it: while reason leads to conclusions, emotions lead to actions.

Aqua "I Feel Good" television commercial, Indonesia.

What part does Mystery play in the Lovemarks Story?

V. SHANTAKUMAR India is a country of myths, legends, and stories. We find that brands that have a story or a legend around them are often better accepted. A terrific example is India's second-largest telecom player, Reliance Infocomm. The late founder of this group, Dhirubhai Ambani, was a simple man of the large Indian middle class. Like millions of others he had big dreams of making it to the top. But with Dhirubhai Ambani there was one big difference: he had the vision and caliber to match.

In 1999, when he was already being hailed as one of India's greatest businessmen, Dhirubhai started Reliance Infocomm. His vision was to make mobile telephony accessible to every Indian. As Dhirubhai said, "If a simple postcard costs 40 paise to mail, why shouldn't mobile telephony be just as affordable?" Every Indian, on every rung of the economic ladder, was offered a chance to go mobile with a product that is world-class in every respect—technology, service, style.

The first set of campaign communications declared, "Here is Dhirubhai's dream, now come be a part of it." Dhirubhai, his life and his dream, broke class barriers because workmen and executives could all afford mobile telephony. For many, the Reliance mobile hand phone was the first telephone they had owned in their life. And so a whole new group of Indians entered the communication era.

PEDRO SIMKO People love stories, they love the way the past can be brought into the present and comment on the future. They love to dream and they want to be inspired. And they love Mystery. E.M.Forster wrote over a century ago: "Make sure you don't tell her everything about you on your first date." How right he was. We're intrigued and seduced by what we don't know—we love Mystery.

A perfect example is the little owls we created for Cardinal Beer in Switzerland. As soon as the campaign was out, we got calls from journalists, friends, and consumers. Everyone wanted to know whether the owls were a couple, or just friends. We said we didn't know and asked them what they thought! Soon the client was inundated with mail—everyone had a theory on the owls. Even now, four years after the launch, it is still Switzerland's most-loved beer campaign!

Cardinal Beer "Owls" television commercial, Switzerland.

One of them is wearing dentures.

But which one?

Fixodent "Which one?" television commercial, Italy.

And Intimacy, how does this fit into the picture?

CAROL MILLER REPETTO You don't get a much more intimate situation than wearing dentures. In our work with Fixodent we have taken the brand beyond the old problem/solution paradigm, from being about how to avoid painful social situations to giving consumers back their emotional lives. How did we do that? By acknowledging the importance of Intimacy. We listened to our consumers and acknowledged that what they told us about their desire to participate fully in life was important.

In response we offered them a real emotional life from a brand that was iconic but low on the radar. Fixodent was a brand people did not want to be seen in the aisle purchasing. It served to help hide consumers' "dirty little secret." By elevating the brand beyond a functional solution we de-stigmatized wearing dentures.

Picking up on the power of Intimacy, our current campaign is called "No Difference." The idea being that there is no difference between a person who wears dentures from a person who doesn't. A current execution of it is called "Kiss." It features consumers in this intimate and emotional act and puts the question, "One of these people is wearing dentures—but which one?" We believe that this is the sort of emotional reality that can transform Fixodent into a Lovemark.

JOHN BOWMAN Lovemarks are wellsprings of stories that their consumers share. They are powerful tales that touch hearts and enrich lives. We've found Cheerios to be a never-ending source of deeply-felt life experiences. It is often the first finger food many parents share with their children. We based a television commercial on this moment.

The importance of this first contact was highlighted in the experiences of couples who traveled from the United States to Russia to adopt children they had never met, and who did not speak English. Because it was the language of the heart, the language of Cheerios proved to be universal.

The result was heartfelt scenes highlighting the touching connections being made between parents and their newly-adopted children. As the parents and children played with the Cheerios and ate them one by one on the long trip to their new home, they created an Intimacy that would last them a lifetime. The message that brought this wonderful adoption story to the public, in theaters and on TV, was inspired by unsolicited true-life letters that were sent to General Mills.

Cheerios "Adoption" television commercial,
United States.

ЗАКОН ЖИЗНИ   **ЗАКОН FOSTER'S**

ЖИВИ ПО-АВСТРАЛИЙСКИ!   **F FOSTER'S**

ЧРЕЗМЕРНОЕ УПОТРЕБЛЕНИЕ ПИВА МОЖЕТ ПОВРЕДИТЬ ЗДОРОВЬЮ

Foster's "Life's Law; Foster's Law. Live Australian!" print and billboard advertisements, Russia.

JANE WAGNER I think if we are going to create ideas that can "get intimate" with people, we have to understand what causes emotional reactions and responses to a brand. You have to get really personal and you have to ask questions like: What touches you? What makes you cry? What makes you laugh? What kind of laughter is it?

We have found that humor can be very powerful. The world can be a pretty tough place a lot of the time, and making people laugh, especially at themselves, requires empathy and a deep understanding of the human psyche.

In Russia we won the account for the Foster's beer launch by using a simple law of life that made people laugh. Why? Because it made fun of the new beer laws which prevented beer advertisers from using people, animals, or animations of them! We called the campaign "Life's Law; Foster's Law." The idea was that if something in life can go wrong it will, but with Foster's Law things will go the way you want them to.

The campaign has had a great response from the public and, via the Internet, we now have people creating their own "Laws."

How important are the senses?

PEDRO SIMKO For emotions to work, all the senses need to be engaged. In English we say: "I see what you mean," "I hear where you're coming from," "Victory was so close you could taste it."

So creating sounds, smells, tastes, and tactile experiences—not only beautiful images—will make all the difference. We have 1,000 genes allocated to smell and, I'm told, only four to vision. I remember talking to a Bentley dealer who told me that most people who buy a Bentley never even drive the car before they purchase. The sale is made when they climb into the driver's seat and smell it!

JOHN BOWMAN You certainly get all five senses connecting when you have your first cup of coffee in the morning! We all know that coffee drinkers look forward to the first cup to jump-start their day. Our client Folgers has focused on smell as the highest point of arousing the senses. Anticipation begins with aroma and Folgers have evocatively placed "Mountain Grown aroma" in every message for almost 20 years, always putting the irresistible scent of Folgers at the height of the drama.

Helen Keller once said, "Smell is a potent wizard that transports you across thousands of miles and all the years you have lived." By inspiring with this one essential sense, Folgers has created millions of devotees who sing along with the jingle "The best part of wakin' up is Folgers in your cup."

JANE WAGNER Music also lets us get intimate. Far too often music is tacked on at the end as an afterthought and is not treated as an integral part of the idea. We believe that music is universal, especially in our modern world. A single note of music can easily speak a thousand words.

Folgers "Chopper 5" television commercial, United States.

How do you keep the Love in Lovemarks strong?

V. SHANTAKUMAR Love lasts when the relationship is mutually rewarding and fulfilling. We have discovered that needs change as relationships grow, and that Love blooms when it adjusts to changing needs.

Take, for example, the Santro car from Hyundai. It's a compact family car launched in India in 1998, and is on its way to becoming a Lovemark. Because it is the first high-roofed compact car that has been seen on Indian roads, a range of people thought it strange and ugly. There was also the issue that Korean products were not seen as good-quality when compared to Japanese and German cars. And for many people in India, Hyundai was an unpronounceable name!

We started our Lovemarks campaign by sequentially answering the consumer's questions. This process was made all the more memorable and entertaining by the introduction of Shah Rukh Khan—India's reigning heartthrob and cine-star and, according to *Time* magazine, the biggest superstar in the world.

In one of the television commercials we had Shah Rukh Khan making up his mind as to whether he would agree to advertise the car by asking a Korean the same questions the consumer would want answered before she bought the car. From that moment the Santro, Shah Rukh Khan, and the Indian consumer were inextricably linked.

Then, in 2003, we discovered that the brand had moved from vibrant to dependable. We knew we needed to woo consumers back, but at the same time we were conscious that our consumers were asking us for a reason to keep on loving the Santro. To inspire Love we created a concept called "The Sunshine Car" presenting Priety Zinta, a vivacious female star, alongside Shah Rukh Khan. Our research told us the combination was a winner.

ABOVE: *Hyundai Santro "Switzerland" television commercial starring Shah Rukh Khan and Priety Zinta, India.*

JORGE OLLER How do we keep Lovemarks strong? I can answer that very simply because Lovemarks is a powerful idea that transformed my life and my style of leadership. It also changed the way we run the company, and the world of many of our clients. We have touched many people with this idea and, because Lovemarks is a holistic concept, our clients quickly understand how it can reach directly into Human Resources, the Board of Directors, or even into their relationship with the bank. Because Lovemarks requires both Love and Respect, it is recognized as truly transformational.

Harvard Professor Michael Porter wrote that strategy is about choices, trade-offs, and deliberately deciding to be different. I believe that the Lovemarks theory is strategically sound and deeply inspirational. And why is it such a strong influence on us and our clients? Because Lovemarks is contagious and fulfilling, is hard business, and will generate sustainable growth in loyalty, sales, and profits. I personally believe it is an idea that will prevail for at least the next 100 years.

Lights, camera, love

Lovemarks at work

One thing you can count on with Lovemarks is that the great clients get it straight away. They know that Love is more than the new black. It's fundamental: high Love built on a foundation of high Respect. Creative, innovative, and full of great ideas, our people deliver irresistible campaigns alive with Mystery, Sensuality, and Intimacy. The results speak for themselves. This creative outpouring is not just channelled into living rooms via television, it is in the streets, on revolving doors, broadcast on mobile phones, pasted up on lamp posts, and indeed placed anywhere else where it can attract and engage consumers. The images on the following pages show us at work, demonstrating the power of emotional connections.

Here is a selection of ideas that have been created to help great companies take their consumers by the heart. From breathing new life into Pillsbury's Doughboy to parking a Lexus in the driveway of magazine reader's hopes and aspirations. In these pages you'll discover the full spectrum of emotion.

Our campaign undertaken for the National Society for the Prevention of Cruelty to Children will always be remembered as a landmark communications idea with its sophisticated combination of cartoon imagery and real world abuse. Just as moving is our campaign for the Martin Luther King Jr. National Memorial Foundation. As you experience shock followed by sadness and outrage then hope, you too will understand why we believe so strongly in the power of Love. KR

The Whale and Dolphin Conservation Society

Whales and dolphins have always been icons of Mystery. From the furious chase in Melville's *Moby Dick* to whale and dolphin tourist experiences, these seagoing mammals have always struck a powerful chord with humans.

Saatchi & Saatchi understood that any campaign to promote the Whale and Dolphin Conservation Society (WDCS) would have to both acknowledge the iconic stature of whales and dolphins and make an emotional link to the people who might support their protection.

By shaping human hands into the familiar silhouette of a whale's tail, the photograph at the center of the campaign combines Sensuality and Intimacy without losing the Mystery that surrounds these ocean-dwelling creatures.

Saatchi & Saatchi
LONDON

WDCS
Whale & Dolphin Conservation Society

Give. And we can still save the whales.
Visit www.wdcs.org/join to donate.

WE ARE NOT MEANT TO FLY
AND LEAVE OUR SACRED LAND
WE ARE NOT MEANT TO GET
FROM THE TABLES OF OTHERS
WE WILL WORK AND WE WILL SWEAT
AND WE WILL BUILD A HOUSE
OF LAUGHTER AND DREAMS
WE ARE NOT HAPPY 'TIL OUR
feet touch the soil

*Voiceover from Guinness "Poem"
television commercial*

Guinness

Great Lovemarks tap into dreams, bringing the desires and passions of consumers into the real world. Walt Disney once famously said, "If you can dream it you can do it." This was the inspirational message of Guinness "Poem".

Sport has always been charged with emotion, and great sports teams are the very stuff of a country's aspirations. When Guinness wanted to help raise spirits in Nigeria, it was the possibility of participating in soccer's World Cup that they put up as an inspirational challenge.

For Africa to succeed in soccer will take relentless willpower, dedication, and inner strength—attributes closely associated with the Guinness brand. Rather than associate Guinness with the tournament itself Saatchi & Saatchi Cape Town chose to explore the very real depth of the relationship that Africans share with the game. In doing so they saluted Nigeria's resolve to one day show their true potential as world champions.

Saatchi & Saatchi
CAPE TOWN

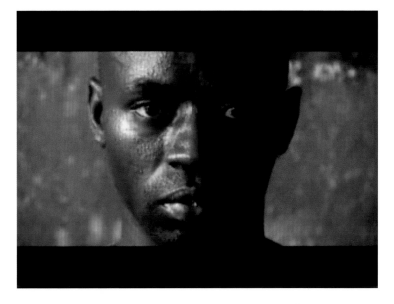

Iams

There are moments in life where
your mind goes on hold, open
to anything that might attract
your attention. Saatchi & Saatchi
selected just such a moment—
waiting for the boom to rise for
your car—to feature the benefit
of Iams. Using the iconic
expression "like a dog with a
bone," the campaign put puppy
passion to work in car parks.
Mystery? Yes. Sensuality? Yes.
Intimacy? Ask the dog.

Saatchi & Saatchi
SYDNEY

STOŁECZNA
ŚRODA
23 listopada 2005
NR 272.4975
NAKŁAD 407 tys.   WAW   2,80 zł
W TYM 7% VAT
5
REDAKTOR PROWADZĄCY
Grzegorz Sroczyński
WYDAJE AGORA SA
NUMER INDEKSU: 350141

NAM NIE JEST WSZYSTKO JEDNO

gazeta
WYBORCZA

OD DZIŚ
W sprzedaży
II tom kolekcji Chopin
Partner kolekcji:
PKO Bank Polski

MINISTER ~~SZYSZKO~~
I ~~————~~ DRWALE

10 mld zł na PZU?

E ureko zażądało wczoraj od Polski gigantycznego odszkodowania – 6 mld zł za odwlekanie prywatyzacji PZU. Chce też akcji PZU – o 4 mld zł taniej, niż wycenia je rynek. Konflikt z inwestorem w PZU, holenderską spółką Eureko.

▬▬▬▬▬▬▬▬

Szczegóły – s. 23

KOMENTARZ
Dominika Wielowieyska

▬▬▬ politycy ▬▬▬

W iele razy pisaliśmy w „Gazecie", że trzeba szybko rozwiązać konflikt z Eureko o akcje PZU – że lepsza jest ugoda niż czekanie na wyrok Międzynarodowego ▬▬▬▬▬▬

▬▬▬▬▬▬▬▬

Eureko ▬▬▬▬▬▬ 10 mld zł. A może od nzu ▬

▬▬▬▬▬▬▬

przedstawi wyliczenia, skąd wzięło te 10 mld. ▬

Dlaczego ▬▬▬ Jan Szyszko broni ▬▬▬

▬▬▬▬ sprawy

P remier Kazimierz Marcinkiewicz wezwał wczoraj wieczorem Szyszkę na rozmowę o Tomaszewskim. – Wciąż uważam, że dopóki człowiek nie jest skazany, jest niewinny – powiedział nam przed rozmową z premierem minister środowiska.
W poniedziałek ujawniliśmy, że Konrad Tomaszewski, za rządów AWS dy▬▬▬▬▬

przekazanie po ▬▬▬▬

▬▬▬▬▬▬

Jan Szyszko, minister ochrony środowiska

▬▬▬▬▬▬

rozpatrzeniem odwołania zaprosili do Kościerzyny Konrada Tomaszewskiego, wówczas wiceszefa Lasów, i Jana Szyszkę, ministra ochrony środowiska. ▬▬▬

Zmniejszenie kary z 800 tys. zł do 13 tys. zł. I odwołanie regionalnego dyrektora Lasów, który wysoką karę nałożył.

pamiętam

– Nie pamiętam tej wizyty, musiałbym sobie przypomnieć, postaram się sprawdzić

Konrad Tomaszewski długo autoryzował swoją wypowiedź: – W toku wykonywanych zadań odbywałem bardzo wiele wyjazdów służbowych, ▬▬▬

▬▬▬ 236 tys. zł.

MAREK STERLINGOW
MAREK WĄS, GDAŃSK

Śmierć górników

Trzech górników zasypały wczoraj kamienie i miał w kopalni Zofiówka w Jastrzębiu Zdroju. Ciała dwóch odnaleziono. Zdaniem ratowników trzeci ma małe szanse na przeżycie.

O wypadku – s. 5

Julia ▬▬▬

P onad 100 tys. ludzi przyszło wczoraj na pl. Niepodległości w centrum Kijowa, by świętować pierwszą rocznicę pomarańczowej rewolucji. ▬▬▬

▬▬▬▬▬▬

Zwolennicy Tymoszenko wniośli ją na plac ▬

Amnesty International

Saatchi & Saatchi used a deceptively simple solution to tackle a complex problem—the silencing of independent journalists and politicians in Belarus. Newspapers *Gazeta Wyborcza* and *Rzeczpospolita* were published with censored front pages and over 20,000 taped posters were put up in Polish streets, while two key internet portals similarly "censored" their news. Combining the sense of touch with the suppression of sound created a campaign that spoke volumes through silence.

Saatchi & Saatchi
POLAND

Campana Brothers

When brothers Fernando and Humberto Campana decided to share their creative process on the internet they wanted it to reflect their personalities. Since 1984, the brothers—two of Brazil's most famous designers with a growing global reputation—have been making furniture created from everyday materials and inspired by Brazilian street life culture, from the suburbs to the rich neighbourhoods. The Campana Brothers website needed to be startlingly simple and passionately complex—a mixture of fairy tale, poetry, and whimsical storytelling. Working closely with the brothers, Saatchi & Saatchi helped create an internet experience that gave consumers access to both the work and the imaginative world of Campana.

www.campanabrothers.com

F/Nazca
Saatchi & Saatchi
BRAZIL

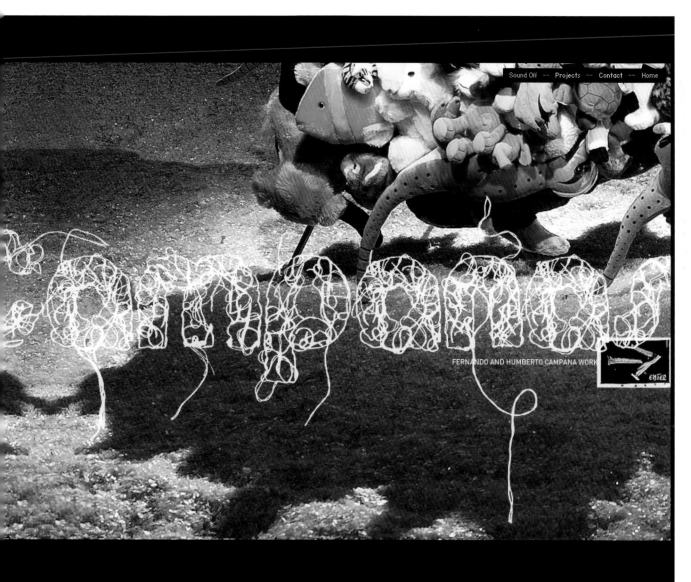

Sound Off -- Projects -- Contact -- Home

FERNANDO AND HUMBERTO CAMPANA WORK

ENTER

Martin Luther King Jr.
National Memorial Project Foundation

America 1963: a white world was transformed into color by a man who dared to dream. Martin Luther King Jr. stood up for what he believed, and today the results are far-reaching. The signs bearing messages like "For Whites Only" have been relegated to museums and garbage cans.

These divisive placards were relived in the 2005 Build the Dream campaign as a frightening reminder of what the world would have been like had Dr. King not acted against injustice. The Martin Luther King Jr. National Memorial Project Foundation's aim for the campaign was to raise money for a Washington DC memorial to the man.

The television and print ads for the campaign juxtapose the contentious messages with modern day scenarios—on ATMs, children's rides, phones, and in rest rooms.

Where would the world be without the man who had a dream? In black-and-white, not technicolor.

Saatchi & Saatchi
NEW YORK

WHERE WOULD WE BE IF MARTIN LUTHER KING ONLY PREACHED ON SUNDAYS?

Regardless of color, religion, or ethnicity, Martin Luther King, Jr., believed in equality for all Americans. Now it's our turn to keep his dream of hope alive. Help build The Martin Luther King, Jr. National Memorial on the Mall in Washington, DC. Your support will help future generations learn that without the tireless work of Dr. King, the world they live in could be a very different place.

MARTIN LUTHER KING JR. · NATIONAL MEMORIAL · WASHINGTON DC

CALL 1 888 4-THE DREAM or VISIT BUILDTHEDREAM.ORG

Lexus

OUR BEST DEFENSES
AGAINST NATURE'S WORST OFFENSES.

The air filtration in most automobiles screens out particles, and not much else. So pollen, mold, bacteria and odors still have a chance of getting through. To combat this, Lexus engineers have implemented purifying technology you'd be more likely to find in a hospital or high-tech clean room than in a car. First, air passes through micron filtration. Then it is exposed to ultraviolet light, which virtually breaks down the tiniest offenders, even odors. Leaving you to breathe some of the cleanest air available on Earth. For more on our pursuit of perfection, please visit lexus.com

Print advertising for automobiles rarely strays from a well-oiled formula: gleaming cars weaving through tight mountain passes and picturesque valleys, or heavily-polished models sitting pretty under a bold black headline. The theme is performance without emotion.

However, extensive research by Team One USA, Saatchi & Saatchi's specialist Lexus agency, discovered that most consumers weren't able to differentiate between auto brands, let alone amongst the most prestigious.

To break out of the "performance" mold, Lexus commissioned a campaign that treated the car with the Love usually accorded to fashion labels. The result is

INTUITIVE CLIMATE CONTROL **THE GREAT EQUALIZER.**

When it comes to temperature, the environment outside your car is not always created equal. Which is why we evened the score with our intuitive climate control in the LS. Strategically placed solar and temperature sensors detect hot or cool spots inside, and automatically direct airflow from the vents to those areas. Thereby ensuring a more comfortable ride for you and your passengers. It's yet another way the pursuit of perfection lives from mile to mile. For additional insight on what makes a Lexus a Lexus, please visit lexus.com.

Ⓛ LEXUS

not only beautiful, but modern and sleek. The Lexus magazine work called for such crispness and simplicity of production that the ad looked like it had just stepped off a television screen.

The campaign also confirmed Lexus as the number one luxury car in the United States, a position that was unthinkable for a Japanese car when it was launched in 1989. Now, 17 years on, the Lexus is clearly a Lovemark for many of its owners, and regarded as a benchmark for luxury in the American automotive market.

Team One
LOS ANGELES

ON-ROAD,
OFF-ROAD AND
OUR QUEST
TO ELIMINATE
THE DIFFERENCE.

Until now, if you wanted an SUV, you had to
make a choice between off-road capability
or a carlike ride. But the engineers at Lexus
have developed a new technology called the
Kinetic Dynamic Suspension System (KDSS)*
that senses the type of terrain you're on and
then helps to give you the best ride possible.
On pavement, the stiffer suspension mode
lets you hug those corners. Venture off-road
and now you have sufficient wheel travel to
make molehills out of mountains. For once,
the best of both worlds is more than a mere
cliché. To learn more about our pursuit
of perfection, please visit us at lexus.com.

Enel Gas

How do you help a commodity become a Lovemark? By making it loveable.

Gas had always been presented as a simple price choice against the competition. Saatchi & Saatchi were asked to make Enel "more emotional in a way that would make more people appreciate it." So our office took Enel straight to the heart, literally.

By presenting Enel Gas as a heart-shaped icon, the campaign produced an image that was both intimate and mysterious. Using the image of a heart on fire meant Enel was able to speak both to the passion people have for cooking with gas, and the sensual warmth gas brings into consumers' lives.

Saatchi & Saatchi
ROME

Telecom New Zealand

Telecom New Zealand introduced a new high-end mobile network into a highly competitive market. Telecom wanted to ensure that consumers understood the benefits. We stepped away from the tech-talk, and went for warmth, humor, and emotion to introduce the T3G generation of mobile services.

Instead of explanations of leading-edge high-tech services, the campaign showed T3G services in use by a small, smart, fast kid— Fast Eddie. In a series of television commercials and print images, Fast Eddie made telecommunications fun. Playing on the mysterious powers of sophisticated technology, Eddie's easy mastery was reassuring. With his responses comically accelerated, Fast Eddie made the benefits of speed come alive.

Thanks to Fast Eddie the entire T3G campaign increased awareness and produced a return on investment at a ratio of 2:1.

Saatchi & Saatchi
AUCKLAND

Doughboy

Nearly 40 years ago one of the most beloved characters in advertising history burst onto the scene. The Pillsbury Doughboy jumped out of a tube of biscuit dough and sang his way into people's hearts. Everyone felt like giving him a little poke in his belly just to hear him giggle in appreciation. In 1972 a Doughboy doll was so popular it was named Toy of the Year by *Playthings* magazine.

Thirty years on, the Pillsbury Doughboy's magic is just as strong. After some years in a minor role the Doughboy has been brought back to center stage. Accompanied by his signature line, "Add a little love," the Pillsbury Doughboy is inviting a whole new generation of cooks to fall in love with him and "Put a little lovin' in your oven." Proof that a great icon can touch hearts over different generations. The emotional pull of these Lovemark icons can cut through technological and social changes and speak directly to the heart.

Saatchi & Saatchi
NEW YORK

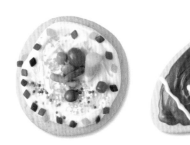
Aspiring artist, age 6

Rookie, age 9

Soprano, age 12

Thankful, age 39

If you can think it, you can dough it. Just roll, shape and bake. Then top with imagination.
Go to pillsbury.com for recipes and inspiration. **Add a little love.**™

NSPCC National Society for the Prevention of Cruelty to Children

Real children
don't bounce back

When an endearing cartoon character struggling with child abuse was aired on a television commercial in the United Kingdom, people sat up and took notice. Acclimatized to traditional campaigns of bashed and bruised children, viewers had their eyes and minds roused from the drone of mainstream advertising.

True to cartoon form, the animated boy bounces back after being repeatedly beaten by his father. The closing frames deliver the final blow: a real child's broken body lies splayed across the stairs. As well as being a visceral experience, the advertisement was also a standout success.

After the campaign launch 81 percent of those surveyed agreed that the advertisements would make them more willing to seek help and advice if they thought a child was being abused; 72 percent thought the ads would change how people behave; and, above all, NSPCC experienced a 100 percent increase in calls to their helpline. Since its debut the ad has also won a string of top advertising awards.

Saatchi & Saatchi
LONDON

GALA 2005
Joffrey Ballet School
TICKETS: 212-254-8520

Joffrey Ballet School

The Joffrey Ballet was formed in 1956 as a small group of dancers under the inspired leadership of Robert Joffrey and Gerald Arpino. Since their early tours of America, the company has become a national treasure and won many awards. Recently they were the subject of a film by the acclaimed director Robert Altman. To help celebrate the Joffrey Ballet's first 50 years of dance, Saatchi & Saatchi proposed a campaign that would put ballet into the heart of New York City.

After photographing one of the company's dancers on pointe, transparent panels of the image were created and placed on the glass revolving doors in a busy inner-city office building. The result was astonishing. As people arrived for work in the morning they were greeted at the door by a pirouetting dancer from the Joffrey Ballet. Memorable, interactive, and intimate.

Saatchi & Saatchi
NEW YORK

KS
HI Project

from
macy.
on, a
f. It

Think about the last time your business celebrated a success. If it was more than six months ago, do something about it.

Get personal. Do you know the names of the partners of your top five customers? If you don't, start now.

Check out an evening full of television ads. Are they emotionally compelling? If not, how would you change them?

Ask everyone you meet for their best idea that never happened.

Think of the latest fad on the block. How could you turn it from a fad to a Lovemark by developing long-term Respect?

Before we go

LOVEMARKS FUTURE

Like all good relationships,
Lovemarks need care and
attention. Here are some final
thoughts on keeping the love alive.

A FUTURE BUILT ON

Whether I'm at a book launch, giving presentations, or in casual conversations, one thing jumps out—people get Lovemarks. Sometimes it takes businesses a little longer but, in my experience, Lovemarks makes instant sense to consumers around the world.

What is the magic ingredient that brings Mystery, Sensuality, and Intimacy together in a way that makes this immediate emotional connection? It's simple—stories.

Lovemarks sail on a huge wave of consumer stories. We see this in action every day on lovemarks.com. People are delighted at the chance to tell their stories about the brands they love.

The ability to tell compelling stories will be the game-breaker of twenty-first century marketing. Why is this? Because stories are the great human connectors and attractors.

It is the difference between getting brand attention using information, and creating an attraction for a consumer with stories.

rks

GETTING ATTENTION WITH INFORMATION	CREATING ATTRACTION WITH STORIES
OBVIOUS	MYSTERIOUS
DEMANDING	ATTENTIVE
PROMOTIONAL	EMOTIONAL
STATIC	DRAMATIC
TABLES	FABLES
LOUD	INTIMATE
PRICE WAR SALES	COMPELLING TALES
RATIONAL	PASSIONATE
CHECK LISTS	CAST OF CHARACTERS

Some of the greatest stories of the last century captured on film. From top: Gone with the Wind, The Wizard of Oz, Superman, Butch Cassidy and the Sundance Kid, King Kong, and Mutiny on the Bounty.

When you look at it like that, it's not even a fair fight. Why have marketers spent so much time shouting information at consumers when we could have invited them to gather around the campfire and share stories?

Great stories are great connectors. They bring together everything that make us the restless, passionate, inquisitive, complex human beings that we are. With stories we can attract people through those "ah-ha" moments, where complicated or unfamiliar ideas suddenly come into focus through their connection with the familiar or the fabulous.

Stories and images on screen will increasingly become the language of our age. Anyone with a digital camera and editing software can mix and match and create fantastic sisomo. Thousands of people are already learning new story skills—as well as new respect for the art of creating them. The surge of sisomo stories created by consumers is a huge phenomenon that will only increase.

I believe we are entering the golden age of the story. The power and inspiration of stories is finally adding Respect to the Love it has always enjoyed. My final advice—test any new idea with three big questions: "What's the story?", "Who's it for?" and "Did you love it?" KR

Frames from the Telecom New Zealand Rubbish Film Festival—people were asked to make a 20 second film using their mobile phone and upload them to rff.co.nz for judging. 400 films were submitted and the site had 1.9 million hits (New Zealand only has a population of 4 million!) Everyone can be a storyteller with sisomo.

Backstage

INDEX AND CREDITS

Index

Credits

With love and thanks to—
Brian and Jane
The brave Barrs
Carla, Richard, and Jessica
Simone and Ben
Daniel, Craig, and Sara
Anna and Sarah
Mark and Sue
—Merci

PHOTOGRAPHY

All photography by Melissa Collow,
Orinoco Design and Photography, except:

p39: Japanese women using cellphones, J. Romanov; Screen monitor at Barcelona Olympics, 1992, ©Wally McNamee/Corbis; England vs New Zealand, 2005, ©Leo Mason/Corbis; and Playing games in a video arcade, ©DiMaggio/Kalish/Corbis

p59: Photograph of Malcolm Gladwell by Brooke Williams

p63: Coleman® RoadTrip® Grill LXE barbecue courtesy of The Coleman Company Inc.

p64: Shanghai Tang, New York, ©James Leynse/Corbis

p79: Photograph of Benetton family by Oliviero Toscani; photograph of jersey courtesy of Fabrica

p101: Audrey Hepburn in *Breakfast at Tiffany's*, 1961, ©John Springer Collection/Corbis

p111: Photograph of Remo Guiffré by Enzo Amato

p120 & p123: Photographs of Andy Murray and coffee cup by Colleen Tunnicliff

p141: Photograph of Tom Peters by Allison Shirreffs

p149: Mary Quant at her Chelsea home, c.1965, ©Hulton-Deutsch Collection/Corbis

p163: Photograph of Mary Robinson by Catrina Genovese

pp164-165: Suexeeka, Banda Aceh province, Indonesia, ©Spencer Platt/Getty Images

p265: *King Kong*, 1933, ©Bettmann/Corbis; Paul Newman and Robert Redford in *Butch Cassidy and the Sundance Kid*, c.1969, ©Bettmann/Corbis; Clark Gable and Vivian Leigh in *Gone with the Wind*, c.1939, ©Bettmann/Corbis; Bert Lahr, Jack Haley, Judy Garland, and Ray Bolger in *The Wizard of Oz*, 1939, ©John Springer Collection/Corbis; Clark Gable and Charles Laughton in *Mutiny on the Bounty*, 1935, ©Underwood & Underwood/Corbis; and Christopher Reeve in *Superman*, 1977, ©Bettmann/Corbis

and photographs of contributors, Lovemarks launches, and Saatchi & Saatchi work in situ; pages 45, 66-67, 76, 80-81, 87, 91-92, 99, 101, 103-105, 108, 119, 147, 169, 174, 183-184, 225; Diesel bag, p63; Toronto Maple Leafs cap and Xbox console, p65; 3M Post-it® Notes, p106; Huffer jacket, p107; William McDonough, p186; Slingfings bags and Project Daymaker, p187; and Kevin Roberts, endpapers.

All background polaroids from Melissa Collow private collection.

ILLUSTRATIONS

All illustrations by Sarah Maxey, except:

p63: Crayola drawing by Rosie Collins, age 6

pp124-125: Shopping's Emotional Drivers by Rebecca ter Borg

p127: Shopper Attention Zones by Dean Proudfoot

p129: Shopper Passport by Andy Scarth

pp130-131: Dream State by Derek Lockwood and J. Romanov

p154: Great Wall of China by Mat Hunkin

p157: Lovemarks calligraphy by Akiko Crowther

p185: Utterly Butterly moppet reproduced courtesy of Amul

ADVERTISEMENTS

pp213-215: *The New Yorker* covers and "Points of Passion" campaign reproduced courtesy of Condé Nast; all photography for "Points of Passion" campaign by Mark Seliger

p196 & p199: Toyota Corolla advertisements photographed by Max Forsythe

All Saatchi & Saatchi creative work reproduced with client permission.

OTHER TITLES BY SAATCHI & SAATCHI

—*Lovemarks: the future beyond brands*, By Kevin Roberts, CEO Worldwide, Saatchi & Saatchi, Foreword by A. G. Lafley, Procter & Gamble, powerHouse Books, 2004

—*Lovemarks: The Designers' Edition,* Text by Kevin Roberts, CEO Worldwide, Saatchi & Saatchi, Art direction by Derek Lockwood, Worldwide Director of Design, and Roger Kennedy, Director of Typography and Design, Saatchi & Saatchi London, powerHouse Books, 2006

—*sisomo: the future on screen,* By Kevin Roberts, CEO Worldwide, Saatchi & Saatchi, powerHouse Books, 2005

—*One in a Billion: Xploring the New World of China,* By Sandy Thompson, Planning Director New York and Canada, Saatchi & Saatchi, Foreword by Tom Peters, powerHouse Books, 2006

— *La Nouvelle Renaissance*, By Philippe Lentschener, Vice President Europe, Saatchi & Saatchi, Le Cherche-midi Editeur, 2003

—*Social Work,* Edited and designed by Mark Thomson, Foreword by Ed Jones, Creative Director, Saatchi & Saatchi, -273 Publishers, 2000

COMING FROM SAATCHI & SAATCHI

—*World Changing Ideas*, By Bob Isherwood, Worldwide Creative Director, and Richard Myers, Chairman, European Creative Board, Saatchi & Saatchi

© 2006 Saatchi & Saatchi

All rights reserved. No part of this
book may be reproduced in any
manner in any media, or transmitted
by any means whatsoever, electronic
or mechanical (including photocopy,
film or video recording, Internet
posting, or any other information
storage and retrieval system),
without the prior written permission
of the publisher.

Published in the United States
by powerHouse Books, a
division of powerHouse Cultural
Entertainment, Inc.

37 Main Street, Brooklyn, NY 11201
Telephone 212.604.9074
Facsimile 212.366.5247
email: info@powerHouseBooks.com
www.powerHouseBooks.com

Library of Congress Cataloging-in-
Publication Data:

Roberts, Kevin, 1949-
    The lovemarks effect: winning
    in the consumer revolution / by
    Kevin Roberts.--1st ed.
    p. cm.

ISBN 1-57687-267-X

1. Relationship marketing. 2.
Customer services--Management. 3.
Customer relations--Management. 4.
Advertising--Brand name products.
5. Trademarks. I. Title.

HF54155.55.R62 2005
658.8'342--dc22

2005049169

Produced by Saatchi & Saatchi
Art Direction: Anna Brown
Design: Anna Brown & Sarah Maxey

Printing and binding by Midas Printing Inc.

A complete catalog of powerHouse
Books and Limited Editions is available
upon request; please call, write, or
see the effect on our website.

10 9 8 7 6 5 4 3 2

Printed and bound in China